SOMETHING'S GOING ON HERE

D1445996

SOMETHING'S GOING ON HERE

Bob Benson

impact books

Other books by Bob Benson:
LAUGHTER IN THE WALLS MO485
COME SHARE THE BEING MO494

Library of Congress Catalogue Number 76-29334
ISBN 0-914850-77-6

First Edition

Dedication Page

Dedicated to Peg
twenty-five years, five children
one grandson, fourteen jobs,
five pastorates, fifteen moves later...
it caught us by surprise.
We took each other's hand
and clenched them together
until our knuckles were white,
knowing full well that
we might not be able to hold on
in spite of our resolve.
So we relaxed our grip and
gently held hands in
a loving, releasing way
and suddenly, we became
more tightly bound than ever before.
By letting go ... we held on.
By standing back ... we drew closer.
By ceasing to clutch tomorrow ...
there is nothing like today.

Acknowledgements

Chapel and Company, Inc., and Emmanuel Music Company, for **My Pa** by Herbert Martin and Michael Leonard. Copyright © by Chapel and Company, Inc., and Emmanuel Music Company. Used by permission.

Dimension Music for **Give Them All To Jesus** by Bob Benson, Sr., and Phil Johnson. Copyright © 1975 by Dimension Music.

Doubleday and Company, Garden City, New York for **Buckminster Fuller To Children of Earth** by Cam Smith, Copyright © 1972 by Doubleday and Company. Used by permission.

Doubleday and Company, New York, New York for **I Ain't Much, Baby — But I'm All I've Got** by Jess Lair. Copyright © 1969 by Doubleday and Company. Used by permission.

Harcourt, Brace and Jovanovich, New York, New York for **All The King's Men** by Robert Penn Warren. Copyright © 1946 by Harcourt, Brace and World. Used by permission.

Harcourt, Brace and Jovanovich, New York, New York for selections from **The Collected Poems of E. E. Cummings**. Used by permission.

Little-Brown, Inc., Boston, Massachusetts for **Seedtime: A Celebration of Childhood** by Patricia Pratron. Copyright © 1974 by Little-Brown, Inc. Used by permission.

New Pax Music Press for **Second Hand Faith** by Gary Paxton. Copyright © 1975 by New Pax Music Press. Used by permission.

The **New English Bible**, for passages from the New Testament. Copyright © 1961, The Delegates of the Oxford University Press and Syndics of the Cambridge University Press. Used by permission.

Random House Publishers for **Working** by Studs Terkel. Copyright © 1972 by Pantheon Books. Used by Permission.

Table Of Contents

Introduction

There was a time when we won all our wars. There was a time when we came home proudly because we won them for the right reasons. Somewhere along the way, in a restaurant or at a peace conference, someone took away our white hat. They may have taken it inadvertently, but it is gone.

Drugs were once just a problem on some university campus a thousand miles or so away. We thought someone in charge ought to do something about it. Somehow, now the Board of Education can't seem to solve that same problem at the grammar school we pass on our way to work each weekday.

Divorce used to be "out there" in society. Oh, we all had an uncle who was divorced. But he was never really part of the family, so divorce was actually "out there." But somehow it has slipped "in here." "In here" in our churches and "in here" in our homes.

Just about the time we felt that we were getting a reasonable grip on the answers to life, someone began to come up with a whole new list of questions. Suddenly we have become very interested in answers. We want to learn how to be "total women" or "our own best friend" or "better managers" or more fulfilled or less empty or something. Almost anyone or any book that comes along and remotely suggests that we can find out "how" is going to have a wide reception these days.

The answers can come in a variety of ways. There are the "answer-answer" answers. They come in three or four steps. We are told that there are certain basic steps to a particular goal.

One must first do

A

then B

and, finally, C.

If this is done in proper order then

D always happens.

If we persist in attempting to stumble from

B to

A and then to

C

Well, sorry but

D will elude you.

Taken in the exact order, however, the steps always work. Jump hurdle number one. Stride briskly forward and jump number two. Move straight ahead over number three. You will arrive precisely in the place you intended to go. No backup three spaces. No go to jails. No paying rent on Park Place. Do it right the first time and you will always get there. No lost luggage and no late arrivals. There are a lot of people who live like that.

But there are some of us who have this strange bent of mind which doubts that many things "always happen." We prefer to get our help more on a "non-answer" answer basis. We want to hear from someone who admits that he is a fellow struggler. We listen more attentively to someone who is actually plodding along beside us. Since we have not established many absolutes or automatics we are uneasy when the "arrivers" shout back to us about how easily they outdistanced us.

We "non-answer" answer people like to hear someone who tells how he crawled under the first hurdle, admits that he was helped over the second by a compassionate friend, and frankly confesses that he fell over the third one. That account sounds more realistic. It certainly seems more likely the way life comes to us.

This brings me to an irreverent thought—one which I am sure I should be squelching instead of committing to paper. If there are three basic Biblical steps to success in specific areas of life, I am a bit puzzled about the reason God chose to put one of them on page 272 of the Bible, one on page 312 and the last on page 104.

That just seems like a funny way to list a set of absolutes.

I think there are two very heartening things about our day. First, we are all admitting we need some answers. That in itself is encouraging: We are asking. We are seeking. We are knocking. Because of our training or background or personality or a combination of these and other things, we ask in different ways. But we *are* asking.

Just as surely as we are looking in different ways, answers are coming to us in a diversity which reflects the mystery of God Himself. The wonderful thing is that He is making certain that we are receiving and that we are finding and that doors are being opened to us.

I have found that searching for answers is almost as much fun as knowing them. Well, almost. This is a story, a saga of my "seekings" and my "findings."

Much of what I learn is learned at home, so I had better introduce my family right away. You won't know the players if you don't have a program. First—and I really mean first—there's Peg—wife, mother, lover, and pinner of notes on mittens. Then, in order of appearance in and disappearance from our home: Robert, busy husband and advertising executive; Michael, blissfully married ministerial student; Leigh, delightful young-lady-type teenager who walks into doors and walls with matchless grace and beauty; Tom, who at thirteen feels a great responsibility to keep the rest of us laughing; and Patrick who is a solid compassionate citizen at eleven years of age.

My weekdays are spent in association with those who make up our company and who, in various degrees, seem proud to be called "the people at Benson." Together we are in the process of trying to make a living and a point.

Theoretically, my weekends alternate between the rich fellowship of our church and traveling. I speak in a variety of camps, conferences, Texaco station openings and retreats. I go on so many retreats that the family insists that I back out of the door when I leave on Fridays.

This is where I am looking and these are the things I am seeing. Something's going on here.

Chapter One

Chapter One

There Is A Secret

Some time ago I wrote a book entitled **Come Share The Being.** In that book I told about some iris bulbs that had been inadvertently dumped on a hillside in a pile of dirt and straw and rock. In spite of my neglect they had bloomed the following spring.

Early last spring Peg and I were out in our yard showing a friend some of our early spring flowers— crocuses, buttercups, tulips, irises, azaleas. Over in the corner of the fence row, behind some trees, there were some lovely irises blooming that had never bloomed before.

I said to Peggy, "I wonder what got into those crazy things. Why did they finally decide to bloom this year?" Peg, with the sweetest smile, replied as only a wife can, "They must have been reading your book."

There is a wide interest these days in plants and many books have been written about the green thumb. I even saw a self-help book for people with purple thumbs. People may need the book but I doubt that the flowers do.

A few years ago I was in Alabama sharing in a spring retreat with the young adults of a Baptist church. On Saturday afternoon we had some free time. One of the couples at the retreat was in the wholesale flower business. They invited me over to see their greenhouses.

Peg and I love flowers. We have green thumbs—pale green maybe, but green. I was most interested in going. I like the warm, moist smell of a greenhouse. I like everything about a greenhouse.

As we toured the greenhouses, John told me about the various plants and flowers. There must have been a dozen buildings filled with plants that were blooming or about to bloom.

The last hothouse we went into was filled with pots of chrysanthemums that were just beginning to bloom. Before long they would be loading them for the trip to markets in Nashville, where they would be sold for Mother's Day.

I immediately thought that I hated to break the news to John and Brenda. But I know that, in the southeast, mums don't bloom in the spring. They bloom in the fall. You know that. Everybody knows that. They certainly should have known.

Being an honest man—one who refuses to be confused by the facts—I told them that this greenhouse of blooming chrysanthemums just couldn't be, because mums bloom in the fall.

"Let me tell you a secret," John said. "Mums bloom best when the days grow shorter. That's how they know the time is right. About the last of August or early in September they seem to punch each other and say, 'Hey Henrietta, it's time to bloom. The days are getting shorter.' "

"When we want mums for spring sale we plant them early. They need to be covered with blooms when we take them to market. When it is just about time to ship them we go around every afternoon and pull the shades down."

I can just see the poor misguided mums saying to each other, "I can't believe the year has gone by so fast. But the days are getting shorter, Henrietta, and it's time to get on with it."

Now I don't exactly know what to think of someone who makes his living tricking chrysanthemums. But I do know that mums have a secret. They don't have a school for blooming or a manual. They just know it's time.

Don't you wish you had the confidence to believe that when your time comes you will just *know* and you will burst forth in blossom? Wouldn't you like to think that the Psalmist was talking about you when he wrote "He shall be like a tree that brings forth his fruit in his season"?

Mums have a secret.

We usually take our vacation as soon as school is out. I like to be long gone the morning after the last day of school. We just leave self-addressed, stamped envelopes for report cards.

This is a great plan for June but by the last two weeks in August we wish we had waited until the last two weeks in August. We usually try to sneak in a little trip just before school starts. It's nice to be with the kids for just one more long weekend before they go their separate ways for the fall months.

A couple of years ago we were a little later than usual in taking our fall trip. Due to his deep love of education, Mike had gone back to college early. His girlfriend was also returning early. So Peg said, "We'll take Leigh, Tom and Patrick, and let's see if we can take Robert." Robert is our grandson.

She called his mother and it was decided that it would be a fun weekend for Robert. You'd be surprised how quickly a tired mother of a two-year-old and a doting grandmother can come to an agreement.

On the way to the airport Robert kept saying, "We going to the airport to see the airplanes. We not going to get on 'em. We going to see 'em. We going home in the car." But he did get on the plane with us and he loved flying.

Every afternoon in Florida, Robert and his grandfather took a nap—an event the grandfather looked forward to more than Robert did. Peg usually had to bring him over from the beach to bathe the sand off of him and talk him to sleep. I just went to sleep by myself. A little sand never did bother me at nap time.

The hotel where we stayed was an old one and we had one of those high bathtubs that stands on legs. As the water filled the tub, Peg delighted Robert by bringing out all the toys she had brought along for just such emergencies. Peg always takes along plenty of everything when she travels. It's just better to have your stuff with you. You never can tell when your house will be burglarized.

Before she put him into the water, Robert was leaning over the side of the tub playing with the rubber duckie and all the toys. "Gran," he said. He always calls her Gran. With all due respect to the "Mee-maws" of the world, that's not what Peg wanted to be called. She chose "Gran." To tell the truth, I didn't want to be called "Pap-paw" either. We came out alright with "Gran" and "Poppa."

"Gran," he said, "see my tiptoes. I'm standing on 'em."

What makes little boys stand on their tiptoes? It's just something they all do. It is as if God had a meeting with all the little boys and gave them all special instructions.

Little boys have a secret. Remember when you used to stretch and reach out for each new day? Wouldn't it be nice to just kind of *lean into* life again and to trust its goodness? When was it you began to stoop over and hold back? When did you start to play it so close to your vest?

R. Buckminster Fuller is one of the great architect-designer-geniuses of our day. I talked with an architect who had heard him speak. A small group of listeners came to shake his hand after he made a formal speech. Someone asked a question of him and soon they were sitting down listening to the old gentleman. He enthralled them until one o'clock in the morning with his excitement and zest for life. Fuller told them that he was constantly finding new principles or, as he put it, "big comprehensive patterns operating in universe."

Someone compiled a little book called **Buckminster Fuller to Children of Earth.** It is a collection of some of the architect's ideas. Fuller says:

> *Every time man makes a new experiment*
> *he always learns more.*
> *He cannot learn less.*
> *I decided that man as designed*
> *was designed to be an extraordinary success;*
> *his characteristics were just magnificent . . .*
> *and what would be necessary*
> *was really to find out*
> *what were the great comprehensive patterns*
> *operating in the universe.*
> *I'm not trying to imitate nature.*
> *I'm trying to find the principles she's using.*
> *We should do things with wood that the wood*
> *   likes.*
> *There are certain things*
> *it likes to be used for. When I use wood*
> *I make sure it likes what I'm doing to it.*

Something is wonderfully going on here. Mums know it. Little boys know it. Architect-designer-geniuses know it. Paul knew it.

In Colossians Paul writes a simple letter to the little group of believers in the city of Colossae. He is writing to them because they are God's people and his brothers in faith. He is rejoicing for them because he had heard of their faith in Christ Jesus and their love towards all God's people. They had heard this message of the gospel from Epaphras. Epaphras also brought the report back to Paul of their love within the fellowship of the Spirit.

In the first verses of the letter Paul expresses his gratitude and joy for them and assures them that he is praying for them unceasingly. Then he immediately plunges into the center and heart of Christian faith. He tells them of the great intents and purposes of God. He writes of the gospel which has been **proclaimed in the whole creation under heaven.** He relates how he became its servant.

Sometimes Paul writes in bold, positive statements that demand acceptance. But he also has a way of tucking great profound truths into gentle phrases which invite one's heart to stop and stay a while. These phrases must be explored and enjoyed at leisure.

One of those phrases has been ringing in my ears. It has sent me down the way firmly convinced that *something is indeed going on here.* Paul is writing of his call and concludes that his task was to **deliver his message in full; to announce the secret.**

For this result he is laboring. He prays and writes to the Laodocians and the Colossians and even to those who had never set eyes on him. He longs for them to **continue in good heart and in the unity of love, and to come to the full wealth of conviction which understanding brings and to grasp God's secret.**

Now maybe it is fair here to admit that when Paul spoke of the *secret* he was probably referring to the coming of Jesus Christ to redeem us. But I would also have to believe that he was thinking in the greater context of the plans and purposes of God as well.

Everything that we know about or of which we can conceive was caused from something before it. Moisture is drawn from the sea by the sun and it condenses into rain. It falls upon the earth and runs once more into the seas to be lifted up again by the sun. In your mind you begin to trace this *cause and effect* back to its very beginnings. By every rule of logic and thinking there has to be:

> *a first point*
> > *a starting point*
> > *an uncaused cause.*

Despite the horrors of history and the daily headlines of evil, we are constantly reminded that we live in an orderly, intricately designed universe.

> *Atoms throb, cells unite,*
> > *Seeds die to live again in profusion.*
> > *Bodies form and planets turn.*
> > > *Nature is stitched together.*

Scientists, physicists, chemists, researchers everywhere discover principles and purposes that can be counted on to work reliably again and again. It is not an independable *here today, gone tomorrow* environment. Men ground their learning in the integrity of the universe. Water doesn't flow downhill this time and uphill the next. All about us is the basic seal and image of God. Why is it that we who claim to know Him best often seem so unseeing and unbelieving?

A friend of mine was pastoring in a small town in West Virginia. The town was squeezed between the riverbank and the hills. As it grew it had to climb its way up the hillsides.

The church where my friend pastored called me to preach at a revival meeting. I stayed in the guest room of the parsonage. Every morning I would take a walk up into the hills behind the church. I liked to sit on a wall high above the little business district and watch the people below.

I would ask my friend to go with me, but he never did. I sometimes could see him down below as he walked the three blocks to the post office and then back again. I kidded him because he never "looked up into the hills." He just plodded along, looking at the pavement. One day while I was there he found a quarter in the gutter.

He was really proud of that quarter but it reminded me of the story about a man who found a dime on the road when he was a little boy. He was so impressed with getting something for nothing that for the rest of his life he walked with his eyes on the road. After forty years he had picked up nearly thirty-five thousand buttons, more than fifty thousand pins, four dollars in loose change, a bent back and a terrible disposition. Perhaps the greatest tragedy was this man's lack of awareness of all that he missed along the way because he refused to look up from the pavement.

My friend in West Virginia never saw much of the majestic mystery of life, either. As a result, his life was always hemmed in and bounded by the humdrum round of people's failures and the inequities of the system.

Edna St. Vincent Millay must have had people like my friend in mind when she wrote:

The world stands out on either side
No wider than the heart is wide;
Above the world is stretched the sky-
No higher than the soul is high.
The heart can push the sea and land
Farther away on either hand;
The soul can split the sky in two,
And let the face of God shine through.
But east and west will pinch the heart
That cannot keep them pushed apart;
And he whose soul is flat—the sky
Will cave in on him by and by.

We have failed to follow the deep insight of St. Ignatius Loyola who taught his followers:

Seek and find God in all things.

We must learn to see God in sunsets and a friend's touch on the arm. We must find Him in the flames licking around a log in the fireplace and snow blanketing the branches of holly trees outside the study window.

We ignore God in these and a thousand other places where He has nested His secrets. After failing to see Him all week it is no wonder that we spend our hour on Sunday in a padded pew feeling little at all. It is easy to explain why the most striking words of the sermon are "In conclusion." Our greatest response is not to God but to the words, "In closing, shall we stand and sing Hymn 462?"

When all creation becomes a reflection of God to us, when all of reality becomes a sacrament, then our hearts burst forth in joyous worship:

Oh, worship the King, all glorious above
And gratefully sing His wonderful love:
Our shield and defender, the Ancient of days
Pavilioned in splendor, and girded with praise.

Oh, tell of His might, and sing of His grace
Whose robe is the light, whose canopy space
His chariots of wrath the deep thunderclouds
   form,
And dark is His path on the wings of the storm.

Thy bountiful care, what tongue can recite?
It breathes in the air, it shines in the light

*It streams from the hills; it descends to the
   plain
And sweetly distills in the dew and the rain.*

*Frail children of dust, and feeble as frail,
In Thee do we trust nor find Thee to fail
Thy mercies how tender, how firm to the end,
Our Maker, Defender, Redeemer, and Friend.*

The life of faith is a life of searching, but it is also a life
of finding. We are to see God and hear God in the
smiling faces of children, in the steady hum of
machinery, in the tear-strained faces of the sorrowful.
He is to be found in the gliding flight of the sparrow and
the gentle falling of the snowflake. He is present, and
can be found, in the depths of despair and in the
heights of joy. He is there at the brightness of noon and
the blackness of midnight.

Jess Lair once wrote: "Truth and reality and mystery
are like the wind. You can't always tell from which way
it is blowing, but you can know enough to fly your kite."
That is all I want—enough truth and enough reality and
enough of the secret so that things will be better every
day. Better than the day before."

It is seeming to me that the more I can sense God,
the Creator, the more I am able to know and relate to
God the Redeemer. As I begin to realize His
"everywhereness" and His involvement in all things, I
can better see His "particularness" and His intimate
relationship to me. As I see His great plans and His
steady, dependable laws, I realize again His consistent,
steady ways of hoping and planning for me.

Chapter Two

Bookaholic—Two Tremendous Words—
I Wouldn't Have Done that—Let A Committee Do It—
Golden Urns and Traveling Rallies—He Told Everybody

Chapter Two

Hiding Places

When I was a little **boy my dad made** his living selling printing. His job kept him on the road for what seemed like most of the time. The Depression was over, but to support a family of five at that time called for a lot of traveling.

I can remember many Sunday nights when we took him down to catch the Tennessee Central night train to Knoxville. He made the trip so often that he was like part of the crew. One night he missed the train in Nashville and the engineer held the train in Lebanon until we could drive him over.

During those nights when Dad was away, Mother would read to us: John T., who was not much older than I, Laura, the youngest of the three and, of course, me. She would read Robinson Crusoe, Winnie-the-Pooh, Tom Sawyer, Huck Finn, Doctor Doolittle and Peter Rabbit. She read the Bible stories about David, Moses, Abraham and Jesus and the children.

Some nights she was too tired to read so she would tell us stories. She was such a great storyteller that we could almost taste the baby bear's soup.

When Dad was home he would read to us. He loved to read poetry and it was through him that I met Maude Muller, the Highwayman, the hired man and Richard Cory. I also got to know many of Paul Dunbar's characters because Dad liked to read dialect poetry.

Nevah min', Ms' Lucy.
It's just Liza turnin' the chillun in de bed.

These lines are indelibly etched in my memory. Even today when the family gets together, someone always want "Pop-pop" to read about Tom Sawyer and the pain killer or about the Blessing on the Dance.

I suppose I came to love reading naturally. I love books. There is a lot of space in my shelves because I have loaned some of my favorites out and they haven't been returned. But if they all came back I wouldn't have enough room since I have quite a few of other folks' favorites.

I am usually reading several books at a time. You might say I am a "bookaholic." I stash them away all over the house so that wherever I plunk down a book is close by. I sometimes think I should take speed reading, but to me it seems like a sacrilege to figure out a system to devour a book almost instantly.

I have a friend who is a speed reader. You can ask him if he has read almost any book and he'll say, "Yeah, I read it at the bookstore." He's far better read than I am but he doesn't seem to enjoy reading as much as I do. I just don't think it's much of a plan to curl up on a long winter afternoon to spend fourteen minutes with a good book.

So I just read from left to right. Then I put my mind in neutral while I move back to the left. I drop down a line and start back across the page. On a good day I can drop down while I'm backing up. I read every word, long and short. "It's," "to's," "and's," "for's"—I read them all.

I was reading the first chapter of Colossians in my inimitable style and I began to come across some wonderful phrases and word pictures of Christ and His greatness.

> **He is the image of the invisible God:**
> **His is the primary over all created things,**
> **. . . the whole universe was created**
> **through Him and for Him.**
> **And He exists before everything,**
> **. . . and all things are held together by Him.**
> **For in Him the complete being of God,**
> **by God's own choice,**
> **Came to rest in Him.**
> **This is the gospel that has been proclaimed in**
> **The whole church.**

This passage is more than I can begin to understand. But Paul writes in the next few sentences that he was assigned by God to "deliver the message in full" and to "announce the secret that has been hidden for so long." While I certainly don't want to disagree with the Apostle Paul, it does seem to be quite a claim when you use terms like "whole secret" and "message in full."

I took heart when I read on and discovered that Paul said he would tell me *the secret.* I read with mounting interest: **The secret is this:Christ in you, the hope of glory to come. He it is whom we proclaim.**

At times there is a distinct advantage to being a slow reader. If you were just reading the "important" words you would be seeing "Christ"—"hope"—"glory"— "He"—"proclaim." But bumping along from word to word my mind dropped into the hole between "Christ" and "hope" and fell on two tremendous words: *"in you."*

Where is the secret? Where can you go to find it? Is it bigger than a breadbox? Tell me, where is it hidden? *In you.* In you and in me—in common, ordinary, every-day folks like us.

I don't think I would have done that. I don't think that, had I been God, I would have put the secret in us. I'm just certain there are some of you who couldn't be trusted with such important matters. Of course, I trust me and I know that you would certainly do the same. After all, this is my third book. But there are really some strange folks around. I am trying not to think of anyone in particular, but I don't believe I would have included everyone.

Some people don't know how to keep a secret. Peg thinks a secret is something that you tell one person at a time. That's not the worst of it. Some people can't even tell a secret. I heard of a lady who was passing on some very interesting and sensitive news to another lady. The listener was quite intrigued and wanted to know more. "I can't tell you any more," the first lady replied. "I've already told you more than I heard."

Some of us are just not too great at keeping secrets. We don't really lie. We're just like my son, Tom—we remember big. But, despite all our inadequacies, we are the hiding places for the ultimate secret of the universe.

I've been going to the same church all my life. Part of the time I've gone because I wanted to go there. But when I was in high school I really didn't want to go down there to church. In the first place, it just didn't have an accepted, understood name like Methodist or Presbyterian or Baptist. In the second place, it seemed to me that we had all the funny folk in the town.

Some of the first praying I ever remember doing was that one of our good sisters wouldn't shout on the Sunday that our services were being broadcast on the radio. Once every two or three months we were on WSIX.

I don't know whether you know much about shouters or not. There aren't too many of them around anymore. I don't know whether we have come a long way or gone a long way. Some shouters have a warmup time and you can watch them coming to a boil—like a teakettle. You know when they are going to shout.

There was one lady who must have warmed up at home because she just "let go." Usually radio Sunday was a special day for her.

I was certain that everyone at Isaac Litton High School—teachers and students alike—had been listening to the broadcast. I just knew they would be waiting on the front steps to ask me what that war whoop was in the background of our service.

I am older now and I hope somewhat wiser. I have traveled some and, after being in some of your churches, I have decided that God in His wisdom does not put all the weird ones in any one place. He just sprinkles them around everywhere.

One of the ladies in our church is sort of the Official Busybody. I wasn't there the night she was elected, but I suppose she *was* because she *is*. She is good-natured and laughs at herself about it, as if maybe she really shouldn't be so "busy," but she hasn't resigned yet. She tells a good story about a conversation she had with one of our pastors who was leaving.

"Dr. Martin, now tell the truth. Are you going to miss me when you're gone?" she asked. He replied, with the reckless abandon of a preacher who already has his next assignment, "Heavens, no! There's one like you in every church!"

I was talking about our Official Busybody with a group of people from a church in a little town up in the northwest—Pilot Rock, Washington. They felt that their church was too small to have an Official Busybody, but they said they would go home and take turns.

Folks are folks, aren't they? In a way we like to major on our differences. We worship differently. We sing different kinds of songs and hymns. I heard a good old southern gospel group singing the other day. The alto sang, "I'll have a new body." Her husband, the bass, was standing right beside her. He sang the next line, "Praise the Lord!"

You probably don't sing that in your church. But in spite of our apparent differences, we are pretty much alike. Tell the truth. Who were you thinking about when I said we had an Official Busybody?

I often think that God must look down and say to Himself or to the angels, "Would you look at what they are doing now?" He must laugh a lot or cry a lot or both. Not only do we do all these dumb, crazy things but we go around telling everybody that it was God's idea in the first place.

I'm spending a little extra time here because I want you to think about the people you know and come in contact with regularly. I know there are a lot of fine people in the world but there are some real "dips" as well. I want you to get a good crowd of them in your mind and just about the time you are ready to give up hope on all of them, I want to remind you again of this truth.

Where is the secret stored? This is the place. God, in His power and riches, could have chosen to have placed the secret about anywhere He so desired. Just think of gold and silver, of rubies and diamonds and pearls, of granite and marble and of lofty mountain peaks. Surely He could have seen that the secret was stored in a more durable, desirable place.

Now, just reach back into your mind and bring out about the most unlikely person you can think of. **Remember: he is the place, the supreme** depository of the great truth of the universe. *The secret is Christ, in you.*

Could I use a word here about God that doesn't quite seem to fit, and yet does? Would you let me say we have a "cool" God? Not "cool" like in cold or indifferent, but "cool" like He is confident in the way things are going to turn out.

I'm not so certain that all of His confidence was placed in us. I am certain that He was sure about the secret. He took the truth and put it within us. He had such confidence in the truth that He thought it would all end up like He wanted it to. Most of us would have taken some kind of precaution to make sure it went the way we meant for it to go, wouldn't we?

Sometimes in my imagination I wonder what would have happened if He had appointed a committee from my church board to pick a place for the secret. I can just hear someone saying, "Let's get a great big golden urn and engrave the secret on it. Then if anyone wants to read it we'll all know right where it is. If we engrave an urn, no one can tamper with the wording. Since God speaks English, we'll putteth it in a beautiful, old English script, something likened unto the King James version."

I have observed the human predicament for a while, and I think I know what would have happened.

Seven or eight blocks from our old office, there is a huge building complex. It is the headquarters of the Baptist Sunday School Board. These buildings, along with one other over on James Robertson Parkway, are the headquarters for most of the departments which **serve over twelve million Southern Baptists. With that** many of them around I want to be careful what I say.

The buildings cover areas of several blocks and are joined by walkways over the streets. There are entrances on Ninth Avenue, Tenth Avenue, Broad Street, Church Street and probably some others I don't know about. Security must be a problem.

If you wish to see someone in the headquarters complex, you have to state your business and whom you wish to see in the lobby before they will give you a badge to proceed. Then they call ahead and warn them that you are on your way. If they are that protective of my good friend, Bill Reynolds, can you imagine what they might do if they had "*the* secret" in a big, gold urn in some room high atop the eighth floor?

It would probably happen about like this:

"Good morning. My name is Bob Benson and I want to go up and see the urn and read the secret."

"That's fine, Mr. 'Vinson'. Could I see your card?"

Since I travel a lot I have all kinds of cards. I pull out

my wallet and show them that I am in the Number One Club. I have found that this means I am usually about third in line and O. J. Simpson is gone before I even get to the counter. I also have an Inner Circle card which assures me of a room with a window that overlooks the kitchen vents.

But they say to me:

> "Mr. Vinson, we mean your Southern Baptist card."

> "No, it's 'Benson', B-E-N-S-O-N. I am not a Southern Baptist. You see, I am a Nazarene. I wanted to read 'the secret' so I came to see the urn."

> "You don't understand, Mr. 'Vincent'. We don't just show that to anyone. The only possible time you might get a glimpse of it would be when we are moving it to Ridgecrest or Glorietta for one of our solemn assemblies. Even then it is quite heavily guarded."

Suppose that, faced with such a situation, I got together with a few of my most trusted friends at church. One night we disguised ourselves to look like Southern Baptists. You know, white shoes and all. We broke into the Ninth Avenue entrance of Southern Baptist headquarters and ripped off the urn. We rushed to Kansas City to put it where it belonged in the first place. If it were at our headquarters we could decide whether we thought Southern Baptists ought to see it or not.

While we were going through St. Louis a group of Lutherans who had dressed up like Nazarenes—black socks and everything—crowded us off the road and, before we could resist, had just plain "stolen" the urn from us rightful owners.

I don't know how the word spread so quickly, but before they could get across the city someone from the headquarters of the United Pentecostal Church got a group together and instructed them to be very quiet. Everyone had to promise not to raise their hands in the air. In fact, it would be better if they all kept them in their pockets unless they were actually driving or carrying the urn.

To tell you the truth, I don't know where the urn is now. Sooner or later it will turn up, I guess. Someone will put it in a tower and build a fence around it and keep other people from seeing it. The tower will become a shrine and people will sell tickets to it. You will be able to buy color slides or little gold towers at the concession stand. Somebody will put a "I've been to the tower" sign on your bumper in the parking lot.

Other people will build motels and wax museums and hamburger stands. You can spend your entire vacation right there. Of course, there will be tours so that you can ride by the tower like you can ride by Johnny Cash's house. But you still will not know the secret—because nobody will let you see the urn.

Maybe the committee would think that everyone should hear the secret:

"Obviously they can't all read it for themselves but we can carry it to them. Let's engrave it on a bronze tablet and we'll go all over the country and have big rallies and read the secret to them."

"Great! We can sing and praise the Lord!"

"We can all raise both hands while we sing."

At this point a great amount of discussion took place within the committee. Some felt it would be better to raise only one hand. Still others thought it would be much more dignified to just sing without raising your hands at all.

The "two-handers" quoted from the Psalms about raising your *hands* to the Lord. "See, it's plural," they insisted. The "one-handers" went into the Hebrew meaning of the words and argued very persuasively that when everybody raised one hand it would be plural collectively and this was the proper interpretation of the passage.

Right now the matter of the order or "ardor" of the service surrounding the reading of the secret has been referred back to a sub-committee and the tour is being delayed. For awhile at least, the rallies are not being held and you won't be able to hear the "secret."

Some members of the committee don't even know yet—God told everybody. The secret is "in you." It is not somewhere you can't afford to go. It is not guarded by someone who won't let you see it. It is not the prized possession of some group or committee who will only give you access to the secret if you look, act and dress in a certain way. It is "in you."

Just to keep perspective here, let's interject a beautiful passage from Romans. Paul is quoting the scriptures:

Everyone who invokes the name of the Lord will be saved. How could they invoke one in whom they had no faith? And how could they have faith in one they had never heard of? And how could they hear it without someone to spread the good news?

I certainly am not wanting to downgrade the great mission of the church to "go into all the world and teach all nations." I am reminded of Edward Farrell's statement: "Be careful of what you teach because they may learn." I am not attempting to minimize the responsibility of the believers to share the source and joy of their beliefs.

The great work of the church is sharing and evangelizing and teaching. It is also God's great work. Paul plainly says it was his "task assigned by God . . . to deliver his message in full." He joyfully acknowledges, "This is the gospel which has been proclaimed in the whole creation . . ." In Romans he reminds his readers, "How welcome are the feet of the messengers of good news." He recalls from the Old Testament that "The word is near you; it is upon your lips and in your heart."

I had a couple of kindly old theology professors— one in college and one in seminary—who both used a particular term. I guess theologians have their own special sourse of humor because each one laughed when he used it. He would look pleased, as if he had thought it up himself.

The laugh always came when we were discussing what they felt was an obviously erroneous conclusion on the part of the other groups of theologians. The error they taught was that man is so "totally depraved" he cannot even desire to be saved. There is no "deep calling out to deep" within him at all. Since we had already spent sufficient lecture time on the correct understanding of "total depravity" they would refer to this error as "tee total depravity." They smiled this pleased, proud smile.

As you have probably already surmised, I am not a theologian. If I were, I would steadfastly maintain that there is something within us all that sends us through life knocking at doors until we find the central one on which our name is written. That which is calling to us and sending us—that spark of mystery and desire for goodness—is the image of God within us. It is His gracious way of placing the secret "in you."

Chapter Three

Chapter Three

You're Something Else

Several months ago we were at a company convention at Lake Barkley, Kentucky. I was in the lobby and a gentleman with whom we do business came in with his family. We stopped to visit. As we talked his youngest son made a bee-line to the gift shop. The father introduced me to his wife, his son and daughter- in-law, and his teenage daughter.

Suddenly the young boy came out of the shop. His dad said, "Robbie, meet Mr. Benson." He gave me a quick, cursory nod as he headed straight for his father. He stood in front of him and stretched out his hand. In his hand were a quarter, a dime, a nickel and three pennies.

"Dad, can you make a dollar out of this?" he asked.

Of course, the entire family dug into their pockets. By the time Robbie started back to the shop he had about a dollar and seventy-five cents.

In many ways our generation seems a lot like Robbie was that day—hand outstretched and fifty-seven cents short. It is very possible that this generation is no more needy or inadequate than those before it. We are probably just more ready to discuss our weaknesses and failures.

Our kids don't always think that our Great American Dream is so great anymore. Maybe we can't win our wars like we used to? Perhaps it is television which confronts us so vividly with people's inability to cope with life's situations.

It is really amazing what people are ready and willing to discuss with others in public forums or chance meetings with strangers. Some cities have radio programs which are set up to allow the listeners to call in on the air. They can say almost anything they wish to large audiences of people. The listeners seem to find this recital of the woes of other people very interesting.

Someone will be driving along in his car when he tunes in to a "talk" program. He pulls over to a phone booth, calls in, gives his name, and asks for the answers to some of the most intimate problems and questions you can imagine. A disc jockey, whose credentials for counseling are a resonant voice and the ability to think on his seat, gives the panacea to all who listen.

Most of us would rather write to Dear Abby. At least

she will print only your initials or give you some crazy title that will preserve your anonimity. The success of her column shows that millions of people don't think everything is going well for them and they don't mind revealing their problems.

The C.B. radio fad is sweeping the country. Sociologists have various opinions concerning the origin and future of this fad. Marshall McLuhan feels that the automobile was the last bastion of privacy in the individual's life. C.B. radio has taken care of that. Twenty-three channels were not enough so now there are forty! C.B. is a world with a language of its own. This language must be spoken exactly the same by every person who joins the fraternity.

We had a unit left over from one of the company vehicles. Tom and Patrick wanted to have it installed in our Toyota pickup truck, so we did. Tom's "handle" is "Blond Bomber" and Patrick's is "Captain Crunch." I don't think I'll tell you mine because I don't do much talking. I usually just listen because my grammar isn't bad enough to talk on the thing. Besides, when I say "Break, one-nine, break, one-nine," I feel like Flash Gordon or someone left over from a broadcast that gave out secret code rings.

A typical C.B. conversation goes like this:

"Hey there, eighteen wheeler. You got your ears on?"

"Yeah, good buddy."

"This is Loco Joe. I'm going down to the big ol' musical city."

"Well, this is the Kentucky Weasel headed north up the super slab, good buddy. I just wondered how it looks back over your shoulder up toward Derby Town."

"Kentucky Weasel, you can put the hammer down all the way, good buddy. I haven't seen a thing. How about the smokies over your shoulder?"

"Negatory. You've got a clean shot all the way in except for a county mountie rolling north at mile 94."

" 'Preciate it, good buddy. Enjoyed modulating with ya. Talk to you on the flip-flop. This is big ol' ten-four and Loco Joe will be sitting on the side."

A good part of my way back and forth to work is on the "super slab." A lot of the C.B. talk involved traffic conditions— a constant watch on Smokey the Bear, who may be in a plain white wrapper taking pictures and giving out green stamps at mile marker 94. But part of my drive is on a local highway. The talk there takes on a more informal nature.

"Breaker, breaker, one-nine."

"You got it, breaker. Come on back."

"This is the Music Man headed up to old H patch."

"What might be your ten-twenty, Music Man?"

"Uh, I'm down in front of the Holder Center."

"Is that you in the tan pickup truck?"

"Ten-four."

"This is the River Rat. I'm two cars behind you. I'm headed home and me and the old lady going down to Rivergate to shop."

"What time do you leave in the morning?"

" 'Bout seven."

"Well, I enjoyed rachet-jawing with you. I'll give you a shout in the morning. This is the big ol' ten-four. I'm northbound and down."

I am amazed at the things C.B.'ers talk about. They are really things of little consequence except that one human being is reaching out to another. Both parties seem grateful that someone wants to know what they have to do tonight and why they are going to work on Saturday and what time they'll be going. We are flattered that someone recognizes that what we are doing is important, even if it is turning down Saunders Ferry Road or going around behind the house to get to the garage. This recognition is so important that everyone is talking at once. They "walk all over each other" as they say in CBese.

There are other indicators of modern man's search for recognition. Most people are searching for something to clutch that will give them some measure of status. I've noticed at the company that we must be careful in changing the most minor procedure.

For example, one person may have always distributed the mail. For some reason you may give that "prestigious plum" to someone else. Suddenly the new "mail person" looks down on the old "mail person." The old "mail person" looks rained on.

It wasn't the mail delivery at all. Somehow the transition becomes "They used to want me to and now they don't think I'm good enough." If you have to change your "mail person" I would advise promoting him. Then it will be beneath the dignity of his new position to distribute the mail.

Desk placement, the size of the calculator, calling cards, and the age of the typewriter all become important indicators. Status symbols are eagerly sought after.

Some people will go through life telling about the day they shook hands with Bob Hope or the night they rode the elevator with Suzie Somebody. Maybe it isn't much but it's something and something seems hard to come by these days.

To the person with a religious background the question of "status" often centers about "the will of the Lord." Does He really have something special for everyone to do? Everyone knows that He calls ministers and missionaries. But does He call truck drivers and department store clerks? Are some people to be apostles and some to be firemen? Will some people live their lives in the serenity of purpose while the rest remain in perpetual desperation?

You can leave religion out of the matter and the questions are nearly identical. It is just couched in different phrases. Meaninglessness causes the churched and the unchurched to search for meaning and purpose in their lives. We do not just want to give up and say, "That's all there is to it anyway." Back in the corner of everyone's heart there is a faint, insistent cry: "It shouldn't be this way. I ought to be 'in step' with something that would give meaning to my life."

Studs Terkel wrote a book entitled **Working.** I am more interested in reading about that subject than I am interested in participating in it. Terkel spent several months criss-crossing the country and interviewing people about their occupations. He talked with doctors, lawyers, bricklayers, firemen, policemen, clerks, factory workers—an almost endless list of people.

The subtitle of **Working** is "People Talk About What They Do All Day And How They Feel About What They Do." From the hundreds of people he interviewed, he chose about one hundred and twenty. The book is a chronicle of how those people felt about their work. They told what they thought was right about their jobs and what they thought was wrong.

One of the most interesting parts of the book was the chapter in which Terkel told the conclusions he had reached from these interviews. He had expected that the subjects which would be most discussed would be hours, wages, promotions, raises and fringe benefits. But he reflected that the great recurring theme of the interviews was not "how much" but "why." Here are some of his observations:

In all instances, there dangles the impertinent question: Ought not there be an increment, earned though not received, from one's daily work, an acknowledgement of man's being?

For instance, a bricklayer felt that everyone should have something to point to to show their children what they had done. An artist can point to his paintings; a musician can play his songs; a poet can read his poetry. The bricklayer felt his work should be marked so he could say to his son, "See that row of bricks way up there on the forty-second floor of the Empire State Building? I laid those." He wanted something to point to.

I think most of us are looking for a calling, not a job. Most of us have jobs that are too small for our spirits. Jobs are not big enough for people.

I was constantly amazed by the extraordinary dreams of ordinary people.

It (the book) is about a search for daily meaning as well as daily bread, for recognition as well as cause, for astonishment rather than torpor; in short for a sort of a life rather than a Monday through Friday sort of dying. Perhaps immortality too, is part of the quest. To be remembered was the wish, spoken or unspoken, of the heroes and heroines of this book.

These are the comments of people everywhere;
farmers, receptionists, executive secretaries, press
agents, garbage men, policemen, plant managers,
cab drivers, bank tellers, piano tuners, executives,
dentists, lawyers and hundreds more. There has to
be some plan and this is what they seem to be
saying.

Call it the will of God; call it meaning; call it what you
like. There is within everyone a reaching process.
There is an awareness of a higher purpose. There is the
feeling that there is more to us than we have been able
to find.

How can one come to know this purpose for which
so many are searching? At times you feel you have
missed the turn before you ever realized you were on a
journey. Have you gone so far that it seems "There are
no shortcuts back to innocence?" Have you so missed
the purpose we are seeking that you think the
psychiatrist must have been talking to you when he
said, "You don't have an inferiority complex. You are
just plain inferior."

I know that there are some conceited people around.
You run into them on occasion and usually come away
wondering what it is they find to be so exciting about
themselves. But for every one of the conceited people I
meet I encounter a dozen in whom I sense a deep
feeling of failure and inadequacy. I wonder if the
conceited folk aren't about the same as the rest of us.
They are just so busy bragging that we don't notice that
they are bleeding, too.

It is here in the midst of a world of fragmented, inadequate, misguided, striving people that I want to remind you again of those two little words about the secret: *in you.* As you look at yourself and others through these two words you begin to see a dignity and worth. He put the secret *in you.* You're something else!

You. You with the big nose. You with freckles. You with two left feet. You with the bald head. You with the sagging waistline. He put the secret *in you* and, because He did, you have an inherent greatness about you. *Greatness is not something which belongs to us. Greatness is something to which we belong.*

I heard my friend Grady Nutt say something along this line. I'm not certain that he said it first but then, I'm not certain that his real name is Nutt, either. No matter who said it first, it is true: *God don't make no junk.*

God in His wisdom decided that urns, tablets, monuments and shrines were not fit dwelling places for the truth. He did not choose marble, granite, mahogany, or gold. The secret was to be indelibly engraved in the recesses of your heart. The secret brings an inestimable value to you.

During the year when I was a senior in college I started a church in the northeast area of Nashville. I was there largely as a result of someone else's vision and I really wasn't very effective.

We took some walls out of a big house to make a chapel. Peg and I later moved into the back three rooms for the first "home" of our married life. I was young and grew discouraged easily. The people I called on were not particularly interested in coming over to help me. This lack of interest is no reflection on the church. Later on I was equally inept at selling Fuller brushes door-to-door.

Just down the street from the church was a lovely, old Victorian house. It was the home of a long-time friend of my folks. She was elderly and alone and was always glad to see the young parson knock on her door. I was young and alone and I was always glad to see a sympathetic friend. Besides that, I liked the tea and cookies.

One afternoon, shortly after Peg and I were married, Mrs. Payne gave me four lovely crystal glasses. They were even lovelier because she told me that they were the only four remaining of the crystal she received for her own wedding some sixty years earlier. They were thin, beautifully shaped and delicately etched. We still have them at our house.

We decided not to use Mrs. Payne's crystal. As a matter of fact, we decided not to use ours, either. We're saving it for "good," whenever that comes. If using crystal is the basis for judging our married life, we haven't had much "good." Of all the things that were given to us some twenty-five years ago, the crystal is probably the least used. The toaster and the mixer have long since bitten the dust. We could use another linen shower. But the crystal is still there. We just use everyday glasses like you do.

I don't know why, but I like for glasses to match. They're not too expensive so when I buy Christmas gifts I usually end up with a set of glasses. The last thing I do on Christmas Eve, after Peg has gone to bed and after the bikes are put together, is to take all the old glasses out and stand the new ones in neat, orderly rows.

After a few weeks the same thing always begins to happen. Someone will empty the peanut butter jar. Someone else will stick it in the dishwasher. Someone else will put the jar on the shelf. At last, it shows up on the dinner table. There it is—thick and ugly—with part of the label still attached. There is no delicate etching. It doesn't match. It's just a big, old ex-peanut butter jar.

We all know that there are some people who seem to have all the natural graces. They know just what to say and when to say it. They move through life with ease and are like a benediction wherever they go. They are like Mrs. Payne's crystal glasses. Some folks are like that. They are better by nature than others are by grace.

Now, I hate to bring this up. Maybe I don't even need to. I'll just mention it. We all know some folks who are like peanut butter jars. You know—part of the label is hanging on. There's not much grace and beauty about them. They are always blurting out the wrong thing at the wrong time. You would think that by the law of averages they would accidentally say the right thing once in awhile. They are the people who say, "I've always liked that blue dress on you," or "I like that suit better than the ones they're wearing these days."

"You are vessels unto honor," Paul writes. The variety of vessels proves that it is not that we are goblets or peanut butter jars or root beer mugs that matters. The difference proves that the power does not come from us. The power is God's alone.

We are not great because of what we are. We are great because of what we contain. He has made you a "depository of truth." The secret is this: Christ *in you.*

I have a book called **Seedtime** in my library. It is a collection of sayings and writings of kids in kindergarten and the early grades. Reading **Seedtime** makes you pause to wonder if we really increase in wisdom and wonder as we get older.

One little boy, who had older brothers and sisters, told about how he could hardly wait to learn to read and write. I remember when Patrick wanted to know what all those "p's" and "r's" and "g's" spelled. This second grader in **Seedtime** was excited about learning words.

One day the teacher told the class to get their tablets—the ones with the solid wide lines and the dotted lines in the middle so that you can make all the little letters little and the big letters big. They also had the big fat pencils which must be used in an entrance test to the joys of writing. If you can hold one of those things and write they will eventually let you progress to something that fits your hand as well as your pocket.

The teacher told the class to write the letters "m" and "e" on their tablets. When she told the children they had spelled "me" he exclaimed:

> **Just two letters?**
> **M-E?**
> **I couldn't believe it.**
> **I still don't believe it.**

When you begin to realize that God thinks of you, it doesn't seem as if two letters are enough.

Recently I was with a group for a retreat and I suggested that if anyone had any spare time that afternoon they might invent a new word for ME which would have more letters. It ought to be a word that contained all the letters in the alphabet. It should make "super- cali-fragil-istic-expi-ali-docious" seem like an abbreviation.

That night someone brought a new word. If I didn't miscount, it has seventy-seven letters in it. I think she got all the letters except "j," "k," and "z." Glenda Wardlaw's word was

theextraspecialovedbyfatherereallyfullwiththesecretofuniversesomethingreat.

I think the word is probably a bit long to work its way into general usage, but it reminds us of the way we should think of ourselves.

What He thinks of you is a reason for you to celebrate your "me-ness." Here is something to celebrate. I have often thought that we are limited in the number of ways in which we can express our wonder and joy during church or retreats or even privately. I remember the enthusiasm of my kids as they roll down a grassy slope or jump into a pile of leaves that I am raking. I see our puppy running circles in the yard for no apparent reason except the happiness of being alive or the pleasure of feeling the wind in her face.

We ought to have a balloon filled with helium to let go of. We need a hat to throw in the air. We need a whistle to whistle or a horn to blow. Some of us are too old to roll down a hill. We would break something if we leaped into a pile of leaves. But couldn't we run around the block or throw a stone or puff a dandelion? What can we do when we want to celebrate our "me-ness?"

Don't just sit there! Do something! Sing, celebrate, rejoice, hope, jump, run, cry, believe, embrace a friend, hug your kid, kiss your spouse, clap your hands. Whatever, whenever, however—somehow, celebrate your "me-ness."

Because He does.

Chapter Four

This Is The Place

My dad used to have a disconcerting habit. You noticed it when you were talking with him on the phone. Any time he felt that the conversation was dragging or that you weren't giving your full attention, he would burst forth with, "Hello! Hello!" It was his way of reminding you that he was talking to you.

Paul has a unique way of writing. He'll fill a page or two with good stuff. You will just nod your head and say, "Preach it, brother," or "That's good."

Preach it, brother
  That's the truth,
Too bad they're not here to hear it.
  Yes, yes, that's the truth.

Watch out when he gets you agreeing like that. He's usually got you running and he's getting ready to set the hook.

The first two chapters of Colossians are like that. There is just so much rich truth you find yourself in hearty agreement.

> **He is the image of the invisible God . . .**
>> **In Him everything in heaven and earth was created. . .**
> **And He exists before everything. . .**
>> **All things are held together in Him. . .**
> **In Him the complete being of God came to dwell. . .**
>> **I want you to come to the full wealth. . .**
> **Of conviction which understanding brings. . .**
>> **And grasp God's secret.**
> **That secret is Christ Himself;**
>> **In Him lie hidden all God's treasures**
> **Of wisdom and knowledge.**

You agree that is good preaching, don't you? Well, just as you get to saying, "Yes, yes, yes," Paul hits you with a "therefore."

"You believe all these hearty affirmations?"

"Yes."

"Therefore, live your life in union with Him. Be rooted in Him. Be built in Him. Be consolidated in the faith you were taught."

Therefore live your life in Him.

"Therefore" was a flagword with Paul. It means that it is time to quit nodding your head and get your heart and your will involved.

In my slow way of reading I have come across another word which is having a richer and richer meaning to me. A speed reader is going to see "live," "life," "union," "Him." A plodder like me is going to see the "your."

The backdrop against which this secret is to be displayed is *your life*. That is the place where His life is to be manifested. The teachings of Jesus are not some abstract philosophy. They are carved into the struggles and burdens, the triumphs and the failures of life.

It's good for God to have all that power and holiness and majesty and grace. It makes you want to bow down and worship Him. But really, if all this life and power won't work in the context of *your life* then it really doesn't mean much to you, does it? There is no need for Paul to talk of all those matchless qualities and graces of God if they won't work where you are living.

Have you ever bought a lawnmower? The salesman shows you how easily it will start. With just one tug of the cord he starts it right up without so much as a sputter. It starts fine in the store where there is no grass, no mosquitos, no bugs, no sweat. It always starts with the first yank in the store.

But come home some Friday afternoon to mow the grass in a hurry so that you can go fishing on Saturday. You pull and you yank. The mower is just not interested. You discuss the situation with the mower in simple, direct, positive statements that it can understand. Finally, you discover that even a gentle kick won't work. The fact that the mower worked in the store doesn't mean much if it won't work in your yard.

Those words "your life" are increasing in meaning to me. There is a deep sanctity to life. Those were great moments when they rolled Peg down the hall and she groggily asked me if I had seen the baby. The stark sadness of death is the simple awareness that life is over.

Jesus brought the sanctity to life. God decided that men just weren't understanding what He was trying to tell them. He had rolled back the waters. He had sent tablets of stone and bread from heaven. The prophets had preached. People had won battles which had looked like certain defeats. But they just weren't catching on. So Jesus came.

It would seem that Jesus would have built an elaborate palace somewhere. There could have been some ticket-tour system so that you could finally get in to see what was going on with God. You would sit for a few moments on a satin pillow in His presence. You would be served some hot grapes. He would be wearing His royal, purple robe. Of course, you could not ask any questions or talk. Before you could recover from the awe that filled you, some minor official would give you a souvenir map of the palace and some cheap rings with royal insignia on them to take to your kids. The next thing you know you are back on the street trying to cope with life.

When God wanted to show His deepest feelings about us, He sent His Son. Jesus did not live in a castle. He demonstrated God's love in the midst of life at its best and life at its worst. He came into the world in such a way as to say, "I am one of you." Why else would He be born in a manger? It was to say to us that we were never to be surprised at where He turned up in life. Once and for all He was saying, "I am here to be involved in life."

He entered into life wholeheartedly. He identified with it. He put Himself within the limits of life and made no claims of immunity. He joined in exploring its possibilities. He suffered and worked in it. He addressed Himself to the ills of society. He pleaded for the poor and defended those who were attacked. He entered into the disappointments and struggles that are the daily occurences of every man's life. He embraced the world as His own. Into the sweat, dust and tears of life He came.

Jesus was a holy man. But I think we often think this is so because He withdrew from life. There were times when He had to be alone with the Father. But I am beginning to believe that His holiness did not come because He withdrew from life. He was holy because He entered into life at every level.

Some people imagine a Jesus who, when He was confronted with sorrow or sickness, slipped into a phone booth and took off His glasses and put on His God suit. It helps me more to know that He didn't have some sort of spiritual overdrive that lifted Him out of the context of life. He hung in there and wept and bled and talked and healed. He was not less involved with life than we are. He was infinitely more caught up in it.

As I go to work each morning, I come up the hill to where I-65 and I-24 merge. As you top the hill you can see the skyline of Nashville in the distance. It is nearly always interesting to see. Sometimes it is sparkling in the morning sunlight and sometimes, of course, it is shrouded in fog. As all these lanes come together everyone is jockeying for position. I'm trying to stay in the outside lane as long as I can because it is faster. Finally I have to get over in the right lane to catch I-265 around to the office. Other people are trying to do just the opposite. Frankly, I hardly ever pray over the city.

One morning Jesus came riding over the hill from Bethany and looked down on the city of Jerusalem. It was a city that had great meaning to Him. It was a city in which He had preached and healed. It was the city in which He was to die. As He saw the city in the morning mist, His eyes filled with tears and He prayed, "Jerusalem, Jerusalem, how often I would have gathered you to myself, like a mother hen gathers her chicks, but you would not."

Now I ask you, who is the most involved in life? Me, blowing, honking, changing lanes or Jesus, weeping, praying over the city? Jesus loved life and people and flowers and causes and was more aware of them than we are. In that very sacrament of humanity, His dignity and likeness to His Father was magnified. In the process of revealing God to us He also demonstrates that *humanity is possible and desirable.*

You do not have to struggle up to where He is. It is not a question of your achieving enough to merit an audience with Him on a day when He has time. He is not saying to you, "Fill out an application and leave it with the angel in charge of personnel. It won't be necessary for you to call us. We'll call you if there is an opening." Jesus came to say, "It will work in your yard."

I think e. e. cummings grasped the great value that Jesus puts on our lives when he wrote:

> **to be nobody but yourself in a world which is doing its best night and day to make you everybody else—means to fight the hardest battle that any human being can fight and never stop fighting.**

So the great challenge is for you to live *your life* in union with Him. The union is here. This is the place. You are the one. The union will manifest itself in the everyday noise and the crowded streets of *your life*. You can be what you are. You can think what you think. You can have your temper. You can have your will. You can have your emotions. He will bring His life to the union. It is in that life together that you are gently transformed and remade.

I think all the Holy Land Tours are fine. I want to go some day myself. I wouldn't even mind getting enough of my friends to go so that I could go free. To put yourself in the context of Jesus' life must be a thrilling experience. But I think it is infinitely more thrilling to know that He will come to live in the context of yours.

I don't think that we are ever completely able to believe this truth. In our minds we are always dividing life into compartments. There are slots for working and places and times for fun and sections for vacations.

Unfortunately, there are areas for things of which we are not necesarily too proud. It takes some adjustments and compromises to make it these days, doesn't it?

Unconsciously, or maybe even with full intent, we are aiming toward the day when in a different setting and at a more conducive stage in our lives we will be able to enter into this *union with Him.*

I know I could be more holy if it wasn't for certain things that keep going on around my house. All of our bedrooms are on the second floor with the exception of the guest room and half-bath downstairs. Peg and I sleep in one corner and we have a child at present in each of the other three corners.

When you go up the steps you enter a small hall. The first thing you're likely to hear is Patrick playing John Denver. That is not too bad because I like John. I don't think his voice will last if he continues to sing that loud though. Over in the opposite corner, Leigh is playing Janis Ian. I like Janis and I understand that she has to sing at the top of her lungs to be heard over John. But I suppose the thing that makes it hard to adjust is Tom playing the local headache station over the top of the other two. My kids do not have any hearing defects, but I suspect that with our three phonograph-radios going full blast they soon will.

I just know I could be more saintly if I could have a little more peace and a little less music. I just know I could move up closer if KDA-FM were not a 24-hour station. Sometimes I think if I could just ride over the hill on my Honda I could sure be more noble and pure. If I could just get away from it all I could write poetry and dream dreams and pray prayers. I could make my own music if I needed any. My life would be in union with the great sources of creativity and inspiration. I would be so pious and holy. I would probably be bored and lonely, too.

I don't think God especially wants me to be pious and saintly away over on the back of Comer's farm by myself. I think what He would probably really like for me to do most is to treat each of the roomers on my floor with kindness and love mixed with a liberal dose of holiness—even when the music is four decibels above the pain level.

Paul's injunction, then, is to live our lives in the present context of "noise." Fortunately, he did not counsel us to go find a situation where things will be more conducive to being mild-mannered and pious. He doesn't say that when you reach another age and part of your present struggle is over, you can come around to talk with Him. Right now, right where you are—that's where He wants to share your life.

Frankly, there are some places in my life in which it is difficult to believe that He would like to participate. Actually, I am a very kind, quiet, mild- mannered, interested, compassionate, loving individual. I'm sure you have already discovered that in my writing because I have tried to tell you. *Except when I'm mad.*

There is a scale at my house for registering temper. To my shame, I hold the dubious honor of registering the highest reading ever. All outbursts of anger are measured against my record.

Until the boys got to be old enough to carry the garbage out, I had to do it. As you know, the two chief duties of a husband are to bring the money in and carry the garbage out. It was a good day for me when the boys were finally old enough to begin to carry it out and scatter it around on the ground near the cans. They got just enough in the can to entice the neighborhood dogs to turn it over and aid in the distribution process. Such things as pushing the trash down and putting the lid on securely seemed to be taking unfair advantage of the dogs.

I really got tired of picking that stuff up. I was out early one Saturday morning and I don't remember exactly what happened. Something just got all over me. I don't even remember how the lid got on the roof. I really think the can already had that huge dent in it. But now at my house they say, "Is he mad?" "Yeah." "Is he garbage can mad?"

To this day I wish I had not done that. It is difficult to see how God would like to be a participant in the life of anybody who acts like that. But He did not say to me:

> *"Son, when you can get your act together,*
> *When you can stop behaving that way*
> *And start treating the ones*
> *You love the most as if you did,*
> *When you can pick up a little garbage*

> *Without feeling like a first-century martyr,*
> *When you can stop raising your voice*
>   *And throwing garbage can lids on the roof*
> *I might be willing to visit you sometime."*

No, it's always the same. I know He would like for me to quit acting like that. I certainly hope He is succeeding in the process of remaking me. A trash compactor has helped some. But He still desires to come and have union with me. The starting place is in *my life.*

If this scripture means what it seems to, He is softly saying, "I want to be a part of your life. In the retreats and the good services. In your times of honors and accomplishments. I want to be included. When the garbage is on the ground and the supper is late and the cake fell and the washing machine broke and you took it out on your kids or some other innocent bystander. I want to be there. too. When you are pushed and shoved and crowded and you end up striking back. When they call and say it is not working out like you had hoped and you are about as frustrated as can be. When you are just having a good laugh about something and something else comes along and makes you cry and weep. That is where I want to be. It is in the failure, success, joy, sorrow and shame that I want to bring my graces and power to you.

"Your life may be wonderfully good or painfully bad or terribly mediocre. More probably, it is some curious mixture of the three. But let me in."

Live your life in union with Him.

One of the fun things in which I get involved is marrying people. There is always a faint sadness on wedding days because it is a day of endings. There are almost always two women on the second row who are weeping. Often, before the ceremony is over, there are two men sitting there helping with the sobbing. Weddings are also a time of real joy as two people come to pledge their life and love to one another.

Something funny almost always happens at a wedding. Last summer my second son, Michael, married a lovely girl named Gwen. The wedding was held in her church in Colorado Springs. Just as it was time for the candlelighters to come down front it was discovered that there were no wicks in the graceful brass rods which were to be used to light the candles.

All of the wedding party was waiting in the vestibule. Mike and I and the best man were ready to enter the sanctuary from the front. Soon there was a frantic search in progress for two long candles which could be substituted as lighters. The lady who was in charge of the ringbearer and the flower girl joined the others in shaking down the church.

The ringbearer and flower girl finally despaired of waiting and went ahead with the processional. Fortunately, they discovered that they were alone at the altar and returned to join the rest of the group. The incident didn't bother the bride and groom. Mike and Gwen are well on their way to living happily ever after.

One part of the ceremony which couples often wish to include is the lighting of a candle together. This signifies their oneness. Three candles are placed beside the kneeling altar. The large candle in the middle is not lighted. The smaller candles on each side of the center one are burning. One symbolizes the bride; the other is for the groom. After the vows have been spoken and the couple is pronounced to be husband and wife, they kneel. When they rise, each takes his small candle and lights the large one.

I understand their reason for doing this. It is symbolic of two people becoming one. But what happens next always amuses me. When the center candle is lighted the bride and groom blow out the small candles they are holding.

I always want to ask them if they really mean what they are doing. I don't think that I would have married Peggy twenty-five years ago if I had known that, even before the echoes of the vows had faded away, she planned to snuff me out. I hardly think it would have been fair to have had the same intentions for her.

I understand the meaning of the oneness. But the deeper meaning of marriage is that two people become one so that they may each become more than they ever could have alone.

During the first years of our marriage we were struggling through graduate school and pastoring tiny churches. We had two young sons and Peg was working part of the time. It was easy to get into some rather lively discussions about life in general and ours in particular. Sometimes she spoke so loudly that I even had to raise my voice to be heard.

Sometimes I had to remind her of some of her faults and failures. This, of course, was always done in order to help. She always ended such family *dialogue* with the phrase, "You made me what I am!" The truth is that, at any point in marriage, you are in some way responsible for what the other partner is becoming. I think husbands and wives have a perfect right to say, "You are making me what I am."

Someone was commenting on a person's face. A listener said that one is hardly responsible for his face. The reply was that "After forty-five, everyone is responsible for his face."

Well, the years have passed and those early pressures are gone. Peg was a wonderful person then but she is super now. Bright, warm, open—she is like sunshine wherever she goes. She walks through our company and smiles and hugs and talks with everyone. In fact, I wish she would do more smiling and less hugging. Her visit is worth two hundred and fifty dollars for morale alone. I hope you won't tell her that because I get her to do it for a free lunch. The thing that bugs me is that now she never says to me, "You made me what I am."

But I think I helped. And I know that because I was able to get that sweet young thing to say, "I do" to all those questions, I am more than I ever could have been without her. Her deep, unshaken faith in me and her love, so warmly and openly expressed have *made me what I am.* Her sparkling eyes have seen in me things that no one else looked deeply enough to see.

Robert Penn Warren describes this process in his book **All the King's Men:**

> *The person who loves you*
> *has picked you out of the great mass*
> *of uncreated clay which is humanity*
> *to make something out of,*
> *and the poor lumpish clay which is you*
> *wants to find out what it has been made into.*
> *But, at the same time,*
> *you, in the act of loving somebody, become*
> *real, cease to be a part of the continuum*
> *of the uncreated clay and get the*
> *breath of life in you and rise up. So you*
> *create yourself by creating another*
> *person, who, however, has also created you,*
> *picked up the you-chunk of clay out of the*
> *mass. So there are two you's.*
> *the one you yourself created by loving*
> *and the one the beloved creates*
> *by loving you.*

In real *oneness* there is an evergrowing and enriching "twoness." Once again it is your loss because I would sing to you now if you were here. We used to sing a little song in Sunday School called "This Little Light of Mine." The first verse was "I'm gonna let it shine." We held an imaginary candle high. The second verse was "All around the neighborhood, I'm gonna let it shine." We moved the candle around the neighborhood as we sang. Then we would hold the candles close to our faces and sing, "Won't let Satan 'whoof' it out, I'm gonna let it shine."

It is right here that I believe people get mixed up with the real meaning of some words that Jesus used. When we think of words like "commitment" and "surrender" I am afraid that most of us have the idea that one of God's favorite things to do on a rainy afternoon is to figure out ways to "whoof" you out.

In reality, He wants to live in union with you so that out of your oneness with Him you will become far more than you ever dreamed you could be. He wants you to burn brighter and shine farther and illuminate longer than you ever thought was possible.

Chapter Five

Chapter Five

Trust The Processes

Our first son, Robert, wasn't very old and Mike was just a baby when we bought our first camera. Since then we have been through three cameras. We have enough slides to adequately defend ourselves from other people's home movies and slide shows.

I guess a camera really does two things for you. One of them is to allow you to capture the moments of your life. We have some pictures and some slides that are probably worthless to anyone else but to us they are priceless. They are a veritable "Memory Lane" of trips, picnics, graduations, first days for first graders, dogs, houses, first dates and costumes. There are even some pictures of me. If they are a true indicator, my life has been spent largely out of focus. I don't know why they always shake the camera when I am the subject.

The other thing that cameras do is remind you that you cannot capture moments. Each picture gently and firmly reminds you that that moment is gone forever. Maybe we don't always hear its steady cadence like rows of feet on pavement, but time does have its way of marching on. One look at old hairdos, skirt lengths, and automobiles brings gales of laughter to our children. At least they are kind enough not to make direct comments about the respective ages of their parents. From time to time they do ask us to tell them how it was to live *back then*.

In our little town a parade is always a big event. Usually, by the time they get everyone enrolled who has any reason whatsoever for being a participant in the event, we are short on viewers. Fortunately, we are on a busy highway and we can trap a crowd by blocking the bridge.

One of those parade years Leigh was in the Girl Scouts. She really wasn't involved for too long because they didn't give merit badges in the area of some of her stronger interests. Such talents as giggling and telephoning are not necessarily helpful in moving ahead in scouting.

On the day of the parade she was decked out in full regalia. I was ready with the camera as her troop was waiting in formation to begin marching. I have one slide that shows her face. She's the fourth girl over on the third row. As soon as she saw me with the camera, she turned her head and took a half-step backward so she was hidden by the big girl in the second row. The whistle blew and the troop went forward and I have a few more slides of the back of her head.

I ran down in front of the First Baptist Church and tried again and missed. I was too out of breath to make it to the next corner. Time had moved down the main street of Hendersonville. A moment was gone forever.

One of my favorite little poems was written by another "poemist" who found the moments passing him by as well. He wrote:

> *Halfway through shaving, it came—*
> *the word for a poem.*
> *I should have scribbled it*
> *on the mirror with a soapy finger,*
> *or shouted it to my wife in the kitchen,*
> *or muttered it to myself till it ran*
> *in my head like a tune.*
> *But now it's gone with the whiskers*
> *down the drain. Gone forever,*
> *like the girls I never kissed,*
> *and the places I never visited—*
> *the lost lives I never lived.*

Just the other day I took Tom and Patrick over in the neighborhood where I had lived when I was their age. We walked around the yard and I showed them where I had ridden a stick horse across wilderness plains. I told them how I had slain a tribe of attacking Indians single-handedly down by the creek at the edge of the woods.

We drove around my paper route and they wanted to see which way I had walked to school. I showed them Roland Downing's house and Bill Hunt's. We went by A. D. Dumont's place. I used to admire him so much because he was an only child. He seemed to have everything by virtue of not having to share.

Tom and Patrick were really interested. They asked lots of questions about where I had gone sled riding and which trees I liked to climb. But I knew it was over when Tom, with a twinkle of his eye, asked me to show them again which house was George Washington's.

When we begin to recognize that we are to be living our *life in union with Him* we also begin to see that it is lived out in moments. While I know this is not necessarily a profound thought, it seems to be one that we often forget.

Jesus talked about *daily bread.* When I read His words I always find myself looking for deeper meanings. I always have the feeling that there was more to what He said than what I have seen. What He said always had an initial truth to the *right then* listener. For instance, here the disciples had asked Him to teach them to pray. So he gives them this prayer. It is lovely and meaningful. It has been memorized, carved into stone, and set to music from the earliest days of the church. It should be, because it came from His lips.

Still, I wonder why He chose the ideas and petitions that He did for this prayer. I am sure that each phrase has rich significance. So I wonder why He mentions *daily.* We're all so busy earning our *daily bread* that the least He could have done was to let us condense the petition time to weekly. What is He saying ? What are those words He is trying to reveal to us?

They suggest to me that the graces and strengths of God are imparted to us a day at a time. Like the children in the wilderness, we need to learn that the manna is daily. Life is meant to be broken down into manageable parts. We are not to live *our lifetime* in union with Him. That may one day be true. But *daily* is significant because we are to live our *lifetimes* or the *times of our lives* in union with Him.

Today may be our lifetime. Today is what we have. We must not waste its time or its moments in the anticipation of tomorrow. I know there are the values and necessities of preparation for the tasks and demands of a lifetime. I certainly believe in making plans for educating our children, for weddings, for retirement, and all the other issues that will confront us. But none of these are places where we will begin to live. We live now, today, and Jesus is saying, "Pray for this moment. This is the one."

I am always somewhere between amusement and another emotion which will here remain unnamed at announcement time in the morning worship service. I will grudgingly admit that they have to be made, but I always question the wisdom of nearly wrecking this week's worship by telling us all the good things that are **going to be happ**ening next Sunday. In my mind I am thinking that all this good stuff next week will also be interrupted by lengthy descriptions and entreaties for the week after that. Let's eat today's bread today.

It seems to me that He is using the word "daily" to remind us that life comes to us in moments. He also is saying to me that it goes in the same way.

As surely as you cannot write checks on the days that lie ahead, you cannot hoard the past. Sure, you anticipate and hope in the future and rejoice in the memories of the past. The time for doing and living is the time we call today. Life marches by us in a parade of moments.

I have had an awareness of the movement of life for a long time. What I am beginning to faintly see now is that the value of life is in the movement. If we are to find the realities that we seek, we shall find them in the *passing* moments of life.

Christmas is just past. I'm in my little study over the carport. I expect Peg to come out at any time and ask me to take down the Christmas tree. We had a lovely tree this year but I think it is at least a second cousin to a porcupine. I am still nursing the scratches from setting it up. It was a good Christmas, but it was the first one without Mike. He and Gwen came to see us Thanksgiving. It was only right that they went to Colorado to be with her parents for Christmas. They do have a little unfair advantage over us because of the Rockies and the ski slopes being in their back yard.

Last Christmas Mike came home from Oklahoma. We knew at the time that the wedding date was set for June and it would be the last Christmas of its kind. We were especially looking forward to his coming. He always calls from Memphis so that we will know just about exactly when to expect him. About four hours after he called we all drifted toward the playroom because it is close to the driveway. From there we could see him coming down the hill. He drove around the curve by Johnson's pond and came roaring down the drive blowing the horn on his gray Opel for all it was worth. By the time he turned off the motor and got out of the car, we fell on him in a jumble of arms and legs and kisses and hugs. It was a fun time.

You know how Christmases are and how quickly they pass. Wrappings that took days to do are undone in moments. Before you knew it we were all standing by the car again in a jumble of hugs and kisses and prayers. Mike climbed in and started up the hill, and with a honk of the horn he was gone. Forlornly, we went back into the house.

What was it that made the "hellos" just a few short days before so meaningful? It is somehow, in some deep way, involved in the process that also includes the "goodbyes." Mike used to come down that driveway two and three times a day. We didn't go running out the door and fall all over him. If I had it to do over again, I might.

We have always hugged each other. As a family we have always expressed our love readily and openly. But it was different when you knew he was coming back by lunchtime.

I wouldn't have it any other way. It is a joy to see him going to finish his junior year in college, studying for the ministry, nailing up cedar shingles after school (saving his money to marry a lovely girl in June); I wouldn't have kept him home if I could.

But it still hurt. And in the hurt and loneliness there was the deep meaning of the fellowship and love between us all. The "hellos" only have their meanings in the "goodbyes." Being together takes its true perspective in being apart. The meaning is in the two taken together.

One of the great hymns of the church to me is "When I Survey The Wondrous Cross." I guess I like Lowell Mason's tune the best. At least it's the one that I sing to myself the most. The words are from Isaac Watts. There's not a weak phrase in them anywhere. The most descriptive lines to me are "See from His head, His hands, His feet—*Sorrow and love flow mingled down.*" Don't they always? There is no love without sorrow. There is no sorrow without love. They just flow "mingled down" together.

There are lots of reasons why I like living in Middle Tennessee. One of the best things to me is the seasons. Winter and spring, summer and fall—each one saying in its own way that the majesty of life is in its move-ment. Life is divided into moments precisely so they will pass and others take their place. The meaning is caught or lost forever in tiny segments.

Some of those moments are good. If my house were to catch on fire and I knew that everyone was out safely, I would hope for time to make one trip back to bring out what I valued most. One of the things I would get is a little black and white plastic-covered book. The back half of the book is still blank but what is written in the front in a dozen or so different handwritings is invaluable to me.

A few summers ago we decided to take a family vacation. We rented a house for six weeks on Nantucket. I had some work to do at times and I would return home some, but the family stayed up there.

It was a house that just rambled on and there was a lot of space, so we invited a lot of friends and most of our families to come and visit. We had company nearly all the time. To tell you the truth, we finally left the house to whomever wanted to use it the last two weeks. We had to come home to rest.

The day before we started to New England with such happy anticipation, Peggy had bought the little book. She thought we could use it as a diary. The first few entries were things stating times and places we ate and where we spent the night. After we got settled in the house, though, the book began to become something more. It usually stayed in the living room on the coffee table. When it was missing we all knew someone had taken it on a long morning's walk on the beach or over to the harbor in the evening as the fog rolled over the docks and the village. And the book became a book of feelings—feelings about ourselves and each other and God. It became a record of some of the great moments in a group of people's lives. There are entries from those who came and stayed for a time. My father wrote:

> *I perceive that this household*
> *Is a household of love and affection.*
> *It has been moving and stimulating*
> *For "Little Jim" and I*
> *To come out of our shells.*

To have been invited,
To have been wanted was great.
But we are enriched
By having been here
By the warmth and depth of love
That fills the house.

Matt, a friend of my son Mike's since the first grade,
wrote on the eve of his departure:

It is time for me to go.
I guess I am anxious, a bit homesick,
But there is still so much to do.
I have felt the salt air in my face,
And I have breathed the fresh air
As I promised to do in my first entry,
But there is still so much to do.
Not any physical chores,
But rather a task of great magnitude,
For I must pack three weeks of memories
In a little brown travel bag.
All the laughs, punch lines, croquet, volleyball,
soccer and badminton,
The little shops, the "big" price tags,
The strange people,
The cobblestones, and the old church,
The lighthouse and the surf;
They all fit very neatly into one side
But the one item I wanted to take home
In its entirety,
The one item which isn't going to fit . . .
The love.

Suzanne Gaither wrote in her ten-year-old handwriting:

> *There really is*
> *Enough space*
> *To have a little*
> *Quiet place.*

One night Tom, Patrick and I were out by Brant's Point Lighthouse walking along the beach by the Coast Guard Station. The boats and dorms looked like such fun that Tom said he was going to join the Coast Guard someday.

"You'll be living then, won't you Dad? I mean, you won't have a heart attack or something like that, will you?" Tom asked.

"Well, I think I'll be around to see you in your uniform," I answered.

He took my hand and squeezed it for a second and said, "Stay healthy, Dad. Stay healthy."

So the book is a recollection of good times, good memories, good moments. Some of the moments of life seem almost too precious to bear. We clutch them to ourselves in fondest memories.

I have had some good moments. But in the context of the larger family and circle of friends I have also stood in a dirty, crowded room waiting for someone to call the next five names. I have walked into a little cubicle and talked over a phone through wire-reinforced glass that prevented you from even touching the one you loved.

I have placed my hand on the joined hands of my sons and their chosen ones. I have earnestly asked God's favor and pronounced them "man and wife." I have also joined hearts with discouraged, beleagured people who were separated by what seemed to be irreconcilable differences.

I have been in a hospital room when the doctor came and brought the news that further surgery was necessary but it really didn't look too good. I've been there when he left us to try to adjust to the meaning of his words in our combined lives. I have been there when the phone rang and a voice from a distant place has said, "You'd probably better come."

Not all of the moments of life are good. Some of them descend upon us with blows that almost crush us. They beat us to our knees and empty our hearts of all we know as good. We are filled anew with numbness and grief. Some of life's moments are bad.

The thing I am just beginning to catch glimpses of now is the majesty of the process. It is true that some of life's moments are good. It is just as true that some of its moments are bad. But the simple truth I am beginning to realize is that we don't always know the difference. In a way I have not lived long enough to write about this. In another way I have lived too long to remain silent. *We don't always know the difference.*

Of course, there are moments that come that have different meanings to the different people involved. Recently Leigh had her first real in-the-car-without-another-couple-date. She was radiant, to say the least.

If time spent getting ready is any indication of happiness and anticipation, she was a very happy young lady. The boy, a friend of the family, lives two counties away and it was even long distance on the phone. His dad didn't let him call very often and I tried to discourage the whole thing by reminding her that his dad was too cheap for a couple of nine-dollar phone calls twice a day.

But finally he was sixteen and could drive the car the forty-five miles to see Leigh. It was such a happy event that Leigh was putting a severe strain on her "smiler." So why was Peggy crying when they went up the drive? Maybe for some of the same reasons I was.

He was a perfect gentleman. Leigh related later to her mother, not necessarily for publication, that he looked at her tiny hand and said he would be afraid to hold it lest he crush it. She replied with outstretched hand, "Crush it! Crush it!"

I do not believe that we can always properly label the moments that come to us.

Last spring one of my close friends had a very serious heart attack. For a while it really didn't look like he would make it. But he grew better and was finally strong enough for the surgery which is supposed to give him a new lease on life. I was with him in the fall and he was still talking about the experience.

I call him Bo but since he is a District Superintendent and I never know when I might need a church, I'll at least say W. T. We had a conversation that ran something like this:

"W. T., how did you like your heart attack?"

"It scared me to death, almost."

"Would you like to do it again?"

"No!"

"Would you recommend it?"

"Definitely not."

"Does your life mean more to you than it did before?"

"Well, yes."

"You and Nell have always had a beautiful marriage, but now are you closer than ever?"

"Yes."

"How about that new granddaughter?"

"Yes. Did I show you her picture?"

"Do you have a new compassion for people—a deep understanding and sympathy?"

"Yes."

"Do you know the Lord in a richer, deeper fellowship than you had ever realized could be possible?"

"Yes."

"How'd you like your heart attack?"

Silence was his answer.

Neither he nor I would tell you to rush out and have a heart attack. But there is a good majesty in the process. Sometimes the good shines brighter than ever when contrasted with the darkness.

I like the story of Jesus feeding the 5,000. I think He was on the western shore of Galilee and He had been speaking to the multitudes and healing them. He said to His disciples, "Let's get alone for a rest. You're tired. Let's go over to the eastern shore." So they went to the water's edge and the crowd followed. They said, "Goodbye." The crowd waved and said, "Goodbye."

They started across the water in the boat and the people said, "Let's go meet them." They just went around the north shore of the lake. When Jesus and the disciples arrived on the other side the same people who had waved and said, "Goodbye!" were now standing there saying, "Hello!"

Jesus was compassionate. He talked to them and preached to them. He ministered to them that day. It was late in the afternoon and they were all hungry and He found the five loaves and the two fish. It is interesting to note what He did with them. You remember first of all, He blessed them. He took them, lifted them to His Father and He blessed them.

We always like to be blessed, don't we? Just bless me, Lord. It's okay. Just any time you want to, jump right in. Just break right in on anything I'm doing and it'll be okay. Any time you want to Lord, I can take it. I can handle it. Just send it my way. Send me a raise, a new house, whatever. It's okay with me.

Well, sometimes I have to ask Him to be careful. Before I get up to speak I always ask Him to bless to me what I am going to say. If it doesn't move me then it sure isn't going to touch anybody else. However, if He really comes to me I can't talk at all because I cry. So I have to remind Him not to get carried away because I do want to be able to talk.

But nobody was fed because He blessed the loaves and the fish. They were fed because after He blessed them, He broke them. It was some combination of the process between the blessing and the breaking that made them adequate to feed the multitude. It is in that combination. I know we all ask for the blessings, and I don't think we ought to go around asking to be broken. He might do it. Just leave that to Him in His good wisdom and providence.

It is pretty easy in life to label moments and happenings. This is good and this is bad. This is a rich blessing and this is a real setback. But the meaning is somewhere in the combination of the two. It is in the process. It is in the interworkings of the two that the deep meaning and the deep power and the deep beauty of the *union with Him comes through.*

I sometimes have a problem speaking about this. I am sure that someone will be reading this whose heart is literally crushed in sorrow and anguish. It almost seems presumptuous for me to be telling you about your grief and to even suggest that, even though it is so bad now, it will soon be okay.

But these are His promises. He has said He would turn our sorrow into joy. He told the multitudes on the mountain that those who weep are blest, for they shall laugh. I have to believe this for you to believe it for myself.

He never promised there'd only be sunshine—
  He never said there'd be no rain.
He only promised a heart full of singing
  about the very things that once brought pain.
So give them all, give them all
  Give them all to Jesus.
Shattered dreams, wounded hearts, broken
  toys,
Give them all, give them all,
  Give them all to Jesus
He will turn your sorrows into joy.

Chapter Six

Isn't Rock A Fine Word?

In a way, it's too bad I am writing this to you. If I were speaking somewhere and you were in the audience, you would also get to hear me sing. Fortunately, although I cannot speed-read, I can speed-sing.

There is a great old hymn of the church that comes to my mind. It is taken directly from the closing parable of the Sermon on the Mount as recorded in Matthew. If I were before you, I would lift its matchless melody to you.

"The wise man built his house upon the rock, la la la la la la la-la la la. The rains came down and the floods came up, la la la la la la la-la la la."
You remember now, I know.

105

Then, of course, there is the majestic, climatic second verse about how the storms came and the "house came tumbling down." Actually, this verse was the most fun because in Sunday School class we all collapsed on the floor like the foolish man's house. We don't sing it too much in our church because the pews are too close together.

In this parable Jesus tells us very plainly and pointedly what is the rock. "Anyone who hears these teachings of mine and does them is like a wise man whose house will stand the storms and tests of life." The rock is His teaching. The wise man is the man who builds his house upon the rock—His teachings, His word, His principles.

It does not say directly what is the sand. Notice, He has said there are only two places where one may build his life. One of them is safe and the other is not. The safe place is the rock. The reasonable conclusion, then, is that if there is only one rock and it is the Word of God, the sand is anything that is not the rock.

There is just one safe place. There is only one place of permanence. There is only one sure way to make the things you accomplish last. We all are aware that we accomplish precious little, anyway.

How can I make my life part of something that is ongoing and does not die when I die? By "living your life in union with Him" there is a place of permanence. There is the rock. Anything else and everything else is sand.

In a way it is hard to believe that a random illustration used at the end of a sermon preached on a moun-

tainside nearly two thousand years ago by an itinerant
preacher is really an absolute. That was so long ago
and so far away and in such a vastly different society
that one tends not to even give it much consideration
in our complex, technological day.

The headlines of the newspapers and the quiet
tragedies and wounded lives of those you know
seem to underscore its truth more than ever. Even the
lives that are crashing down in your neighborhood or
on your block emphasize again and again that there is
just one rock and all the rest is sand.

Just recently, a fine young comedian and entertainer
took his life. He was surrounded by people who were
there to help. He had already made it big. At his young
age he would just barely have been old enough to vote
a few years ago. Tom wanted to know why he would
do that. I wanted to sing to Tom that there is only one
rock and all the rest is sand.

We like to invent rules and systems and feel there
are newer and more practical ways of going about this
business of making life work. I came across a paper the
other day that I had saved. It was printed in the hand of
an eight-year-old. It was a set of rules for the neighborhood club that had been formed to use the lavish
facilities of a four-by-eight treehouse I had built for the
boys. Complete with trapdoor entrance, the house was
a perfect place for forming a new society.

The list included the colors for the structure which
has yet to be painted. The roof was to be brown, the
outside walls green, the inside walls orange and the

ceiling purple. The color scheme alone was enough to have ended the "new order."

The rules included:

1. No visitors in the clubhouse unless a member is present.
2. Meetings are every Tuesday. (I know for a fact they didn't meet this week.)
3. Dues are 10c.
4. Visitor dues are 5c.
5. Member may forget dues only three times.
6. A fine will be a quarter.

The officers of the newly-formed association tended to follow age order strictly as indicated by:

Mike—President

Jay—Vice President

Leigh—Secretary

Tom—Treasurer

Patrick—Just a person

The minutes of that first meeting were duly signed by the secretary and they are amusing to see and read. I thought of Mike leaving his wife and schooling in Oklahoma City to return each Tuesday for club meetings for the group and of the fact that I remembered that the club never met again after the first meeting. But these future considerations did not rob the situation of a single bit of historical significance when that meeting was in progress.

The real tragedy is that grown-ups also make up little sets of rules and guidelines for life for themselves. Many times they build on premises that set squarely on sand. They have no more chance of succeeding than a neighborhood club of six-, eight-, and ten-year-olds. There is just one rock and everything else is sand.

We were at a convention in Florida recently. We were driving from Sannibel Island across the bridge at Blind Pass onto Captiva Island. A sandbar jutted out from the Captiva side and nearly joined the two islands together. A resident of the islands told Peggy that for a long time the sand bar had been covered with Australian pine trees. One morning after a tropical storm, the sand bar, trees and all, was gone. Some months later, after another storm, the sand bar was back. If it will just sit there a while the trees will be back, too. Australian pines don't need much encouragement. You just plant one and jump back. You probably should run, too. They send roots out in all directions and shoots come from everywhere and soon become trees.

The sand shifts with the currents of the sea. What looks permanent today is gone tomorrow. Sometimes it takes all your hopes and plans with it. Jesus is reminding us here that there is only one rock.

Consciously or unconsciously, people's lives begin to polarize around some area of life. There is the job, the home, family, church. These areas do provide parameters for life. They have meaning that keeps us going. But somehow they must be enjoyed with the constant realization that they are sand.

Some things are, of course, thrust upon us. One such thing is work. Like all sand, it makes subtle, unnoticed changes as we go. Sometimes I think harshly of those who set high goals of financial success and status achievement. It especially bothers me when they are willing to make any sacrifice in terms of time or principle to achieve their stated goals.

A situation comedy on T.V. featured a rich tycoon whose nephew was asking him for a job. He took the nephew over to the window and pointed down thirty stories. His line was intended to be funny: "See all those little people down there? I stepped on everyone of them to get up here." The innocent nephew wondered why he didn't take the elevator.

I don't like the man who told his daughter she didn't know the value of a dollar. I secretly cheered when she reminded him he didn't know the value of a daughter, either.

We all know some people whose goals were right. The sand just blew in all around them. They never did say, "I'm going to work such long, hard hours that I'll never get to be with my family." They didn't say, "I'll never have enough strength left to do something for somebody else because I intended to invest it all in my business or in getting ahead where I am." They didn't plan to and they didn't mean to—it just happened.

Almost before you know it the company keeps you running to win a trip to San Francisco or a place in the Millionaires Club or a new car. In the process you passed up too many of life's values. The next company banquet is for you and for forty-three years of dedicated service they give you the crummy watch with your name on the back. Everyone said, "We'll never forget you. The old company will never be the same." Monday morning someone new is doing a better job at your desk. Two months later someone wonders, "What ever happened to old what's-his-name?" And you went home with a pocketful of sand. But one has to have a job.

Then, of course, there is the stuff of life. It is a common assumption that riches are some combination of cars, clothes, houses and various other trappings of the good life. Some way, though, they are all like carrots dangling on a stick in front of a rabbit. We just never seem to catch up.

A four-dollar tie ties better than a two-dollar tie. So we buy one for six dollars and finance the balance. Then we realize that the six-dollar tie makes the neatest knot and hangs the best so we buy a ten-dollar tie and finance the rest on a three-month pay plan. I don't think God cares what kind of a necktie you wear or whether it has a special little monogram on it to tell everybody you are just a bit better dressed than the "average bear." Sometimes the color combination may make Him squint.

I don't think He is worried about what side of town you live on or how many square feet the house contains. The question, it seems to me, is "How much of you does it take to keep juggling all the payments?"Is there any of you left when it is over?

My secretary recently told me with pride that she and her husband had bought a new house. I was happy for them. I didn't have the heart to remind her that she had just promised someone that once a month until the year 2006 she would send them a given amount of money. But we all have to have a house and a car to get to it and a mower for the grass and so on and so on.

It is a well-known and easily demonstrable fact that you can be uncomfortable in a Cadillac and cold in the best suit made. You can be lonely in a crowd. You can be doing very well and still let those down who have the highest hopes for you and your life. You can appear to be a jolly good fellow and yet make your wife and children so miserable their only solution is to leave you. You can greet the outside with confidence while your own heart is so poor and empty you can scarcely force the grin across your face. Sooner or later, it becomes painfully obvious that real riches aren't always delivered by U.P.S. They are not necessarily to be found on 200-foot lots. They don't always come with side-walled tires. Jesus simply said to be careful where you built the house that was to contain your life. There is only one rock and everything else is sand.

Some people have the ability to work their way through all this clutter and stuff and select whiter, purer sand upon which to build. I suppose I empathize with them. I think that I am a family man. I'm also a scribbler of notes and thoughts on cards, matchbook covers, old envelopes, paper napkins or whatever. I'm always jotting down a thought—whether it is my thought or a good one. My pockets have to be emptied before anything is sent to the dirty clothes basket or to the stack of stuff that Peg is going to take to the cleaners. One night I laid this profound utterance on a table somewhere: "I'm not the one who makes me happy." The next time I saw the note Peggy had written, "Who is?" I wrote back so that she would see it, "You and them and Him."

Peggy and the kids have the deepest, richest meaning to me. The warmest, most sacred places in my heart are reserved for them. Most of me and my noblest dreams kneel in worship and thanksgiving before them in these deep recesses of my heart.

Ten years or so ago now, I had had a long, hard week. It was one of those first warm Saturdays of spring and I spent it in the yard. I was prostrate on the floor feeling my aches, pains and weariness when Leigh came in. She asked me if I knew what daddies were for. I was so tired I couldn't think of a single reason. She said, "Daddies are for Saturday."

When I got upstairs I dragged out a piece of stationery and made a few notes which I came across recently. I wrote to myself then that this little five-year-old would soon begin a cycle of puppy love, boyfriends and going steady that would end with someone asking me, "Who giveth this woman?"

Today is Saturday and I'm not sure where she is in the cycle at the present. I'm casting my vote for puppy love but the boyfriend is here. I still remember the shine on face and the twinkle in eye when she told me what I was for. I have thought of it a lot. But this is just a temporary stop on her journey. Jesus was trying to say to me as gently as He possibly could that most of what we take for granted is really sand.

I'm a family man and I think that family relationships are the purest, cleanest, whitest sand of all. That sand has the least trash and is the best place of all to enjoy the sunlight of God's love. But it is sand.

Last September Peg and I celebrated our twenty-fifth wedding anniversary. Furthermore, I signed over for another hitch. I remember when we set up house-keeping. I remember how we put everything we owned or had into a 4 x 8 trailer with three-foot high rail sides to move to Kansas City to go to Seminary. We pulled the trailer with a borrowed car and Robert lay on a pillow in the back seat. Three years later we had filled the back half of a Bekins Van. I haven't the slightest idea what it would take to move us now. Anyone with any notion of giving me a position in another town would probably do well to purchase a truck line first. Little by little, bit by bit, grain by grain, our lives have gained momentum and we have accumulated more than our share of the relationships, joy and stuff of life as we went.

I would like to write a book and call it *Words I Didn't Used To Like.* The list would include words like "con-fession," "denial," "cross," and certainly "rock"and "sand." For a long time I really wished He had not chosen to call so much of my life that means so much to me "sand."

The reason the title is " . . . *Didn't Used To Like"*

instead of "... *Don't Like"* is that I am beginning to see a little of what it is He was saying to me. Sooner or later I was going to be interested in doing something that mattered. He was gently reminding me of how it could be done. When I got around to it, there is a way to insure the permanence of my accomplishments and it is by building on His teaching. It is not some capricious game that I either win or lose by some stroke of good luck or misfortune.

Sometimes before supper I sit down with the kids while they are watching the evening quiz show. There is some poor lady who has had to struggle all her life for everything she ever had. She is standing there in anguish. She has seven hundred fifty dollars in her hand. The genial host is exhorting her to a nervous breakdown on the spot.

She can either take the money she has (which, incidentally, is more than she ever held in her hand at one time), or she can trade it for a chance to select a box from the stage. The box may hold a check for ten thousand dollars or a can of sardines. The host is encouraging her to choose what seems the best for her and the audience is screaming, "Go for the box, go for the box!" Some briefly attired young thing smiles sweetly at her in her agony and waits eagerly to bring down the box.

Do you want to take a chance on the big one and probably go home with nothing? Or do you want to go home with something and always wonder what would have happened if you had looked in box number 12?

Jesus is not saying, "Step right up and take your chance. Maybe you'll win big but you might spend your lifetime for nothing." Instead He is saying, "There is a rock. You can build upon it. It is the rock today and it will be the rock tomorrow. You will not come to the end of your lifetime only to find you picked an empty box." Isn't "rock" a fine word?

Chapter Seven

Chapter Seven

Tired Arms, Open Hands

Some years ago now my dad rode over on his tractor. He was pulling a trailor full of tools and stuff. James, a man who worked in the yard with him on weekends, was with him. "Boy," he said. I guess he'll call me boy until I'm eighty and I really kind of hope that he does. "Boy, would you like for us to plant you some pine trees?" Since the trees were free and he had a man to dig the holes, I didn't think I could lose. I went in the house and told Peggy we were taking out the sweet gum tree that had been hit by the storm and were replacing it with pine trees.

It took us a while to saw down the gum tree, but planting the pines didn't take long at all. I was thinking in terms of trees and they were planting seedlings.

They just stuck a rod in the ground and packed a little dirt around a "pine tree" that was about as big around as your little finger and eight inches tall. They planted a forest of eight trees for me.

Needless to say, the family had many a good laugh at me about my pine trees. Somebody ran over three of them with the lawn mower. We planted them where you could see them every time you came down the hill by the house. Somebody always laughed about the forest. I usually mumbled something about how they would all want to go to Europe with me on the turpentine money.

Nobody laughs anymore. As you come down the driveway one of the main focal points of our yard is these five lovely pine trees some twenty to thirty feet tall. We have azaleas bedded down in the pine needles under the trees. They are gorgeous, especially in the spring. All year they frame the house and give it a lovely perspective.

We laughed at those seedlings and drove stakes beside them so that we would not mow them down. But at their core they had a determination to live. In the basic conditions of its life every organism knows the discipline of commitment in a very profound and all-encompassing way. The whole existence of that organism depends upon the singleness of this kind of demand. It is the demand for food and for survival.

There is also another step involved here. Each particular form of life maintains itself by submitting to a certain pattern of behavior. This pattern distinguishes it or becomes its "method." The organism must meet the defined conditions if it is to survive. A fish has gills so it must extract its oxygen from water. Men take their oxygen differently because they have lungs instead of gills.

So the truth in all of nature is that there is energy and life available. But that energy is always subject to certain given conditions.

It is here that we must recognize what may be termed the general law of spiritual life. In the experience of mankind, the attitude or act that triggers the release of fresh vigor or vitality is singleness of mind. There must be a surrendering of the very core of one's being to a single end or goal. In Christianity there is always the central, inescapable demand of surrender.

The hardest part about coming to grips with words like "surrender" is that we are taught all along in life that the only things that we really have are those things which we can grasp tightly enough so that no one can take them away from us. Surrender has a relationship to strengthen in our minds only in terms of the one who is being surrendered to. The one who is surrendering is giving in, or saying "uncle" and to our minds he is the weaker of the two.

Life seems to be teaching us that the more you can clutch and hold on to, the stronger you really are. That is where the power lies, in accumulating, gaining, putting together, making deals and hanging on. That is where the power is. Hold. Grasp. Keep. Defend. Protect. Accumulate. Gather. These are the words that indicate strength.

Children go through a stage in life when they become very possessive. It seems as if the backbone of their vocabulary is "no," "me," and "mine." Fortunately, this stage is only temporary. Most of us are out of it by the time we are 82.

When our kids were smaller—about the age of yours when they were doing the same thing—they had a closet full of toys and junk accumulated from Christmases and birthdays past. It would never occur to them to look in there on cold, rainy days when "there was nothing to do." The only time in months they had looked at any of it was when you cleaned out the closet. On that day they brought most of it back from the garage and returned it to its place in the heap on the floor.

Some friends would come over and their little boy would go upstairs to play with yours. The first thing he did was open the closet door. Here was a veritable toy store of things he hadn't seen or played with. The following game begins:

Visiting Team: "I'm going to play with this ball."

Home Team: "Oh no, that's my favorite ball." He promptly grabs it away.

Visiting Team: "I'll put on these guns and holsters and cowboy hat."

Home Team: "Just a minute. Those are mine." He lays down the ball, buckles on the guns, puts on the hat and picks up the ball again.

Visiting Team:"Oh well, I'll just build something
with these Tinkertoys."

Home Team: "You might break those. You'd
better not." He picks up the
Tinkertoys.

Visiting Team:"Look at those cars and trucks! I'll.."

Home Team: "Uh-uh, they're mine." He adds the
cars and trucks to his ever
increasing armload.

Visiting Team:A bit warily now he asks, "May I
ride your tricycle."

Home Team: "Come on, leave my stuff alone."
Now he is sitting on the tricycle with
the hat on his head and the guns
buckled on and his arms tightly
clutching the ball, Tinkertoys, cars
and trucks.

Visiting Team:"I can't play with anything."

Home Team: "My arms are tired."

It is comically tragic to see that, isn't it? He was so
busy holding on to everything that he didn't get to play,
either. He can't enjoy it because he's too busy holding
on for fear someone else might get some of it. When
only Tinkertoys and cars and trucks are involved you
can smile a little. But it is just starkly tragic when we see
adults clutching their spouses and children, their jobs
and their futures, their homes and their cars in such a
jealous, protective grip. They never have time to enjoy

or even have contentment because they are using all their energy just holding on.

I know a set of brothers who operated businesses that had some overlap. Upon retirement, two of the brothers insisted that all the money their business was worth come to them in a sale. This kept the younger men who worked with them from gaining ownership. The business was sold to outsiders who had no pride at all in what the two brothers had done with their lives. The business became the sum total of the last two lines on a balance sheet. It was sold again and again and closed forever. The two brothers hung on and ended up empty-handed.

When it came time for him to retire, the youngest brother fixed it so the young men around him could gain control and ownership of his business in time. The business has prospered and now he has the money from the business. He also has the joy of seeing that for which he worked so hard continuing and fulfilling his dreams. He was willing to let go and now has everything he had before plus more, besides the enjoyment of it all.

Here is life saying that you must hang on. Hold on tight for all you're worth. Here is Jesus saying you must let go. You must hold what you have with an open hand.

We are all caught up in the problem of possessiveness. There is no way to remove possessiveness from our love. The purest love and the most dangerous possessiveness are bound together in a way that keeps us from completely separating them. The two are together—love, the essentially creative force, and possessiveness, the essentially destructive force.

It would have been easier, as John White suggests, if Christians were called to vows of poverty. If we knew it was God's will that none of us own cars, that all of us were allowed precisely two sets of underwear, one set of outerwear and $50 per month rent, one pair of slippers, and one pair of shoes, we would all know where we stood.

Jesus did not make it that easy. He calls us to a quality of life that makes us "detach ourselves without abdicating, to be disinterested but not indifferent, to possess as if not possessing, to have and not be had."

It is in this act of surrender or commitment that the vitality of life is released for the individual. It is in release that true possession comes. Hold on, clutch, grasp and one is continually filled with fear, greed, defensiveness, struggle and anxiety.

Let go. Release. Realize that He who gave "this" will give you something better when "this" is gone away. The deep truth of the scripture is not "Don't care and let go." It is not "Care and hang on." It is "Care and let go."

It isn't what you have that determines your strength now or in the future. It is what you are willing to let go of that is the ultimate test.

There were early days in our marriage when we struggled to share, believing that "in casting our bread upon the waters" we would "find it after many days."

He has made us know that we have only that which we were willing to turn loose. Those things which we have shared are now more richly ours than before. Without our grasping or striving they have come back to us.

This is just a life principle and you can see it work at every level. I have never quite been able to explain it to my own satisfaction, but it thrills me to even try. The best way to know you are built on the rock is to hold the sand with an open hand.

Take your children for instance. You want to hold on to them. Then let go, just let go. You want to lose them for good, hang on. Just tell your teens that they'll do things your way and when they do you'll discuss it with them. In the meantime just ignore them as much as possible. Better still, don't speak at all.

When they want to go to college one place, just say you won't help to pay the bill unless they go where you want. "Over there you're on your own. Over here I'll pay your way." So they go where you say, but they are resentful at you for forcing them and resentful at themselves for letting themselves be forced.

When they get out of college and want to do something besides go into the wallpaper business with you, remind them of all the sacrifices you had to make to get them through. Ask them how they could be so ungracious as to want to live their own lives. Hang on. Clutch. Grasp. Whine. Pout. Don't speak. Don't show any excitement about their plans. Hang on.

Just remember that love can kill as surely as hate does. We have policemen to curb the murderous effects of hate. There is no one to deal with those who smother with love.

Do you want to hold on? Then let go. Jess Lair said a lovely thing in one of his books, "You don't raise kids. You raise carrots. You sponsor kids." They are not yours. Their lives are not a second chance for you to be head majorette, or quarterback, or student body president. You've already had your chance to botch up. Unfortunately, they already know about that.

Let go. Laugh with them. Cry with them. Rejoice with them. Dream with them. But let go. Then when they come down the driveway to see you, you will know the only reason they are coming is because they want to see you. You will begin to realize the deep joy of having what you turned loose.

A couple of Christmases ago now, Robert wrote a poem for us and had it framed. It hangs in the sitting room upstairs and I often stop and read it. Peggy even stoops to suggesting that visitors read it also. In a sort of a cool way, I want to slip it in just here.

Most of the celebrations
that I remember well at all
took place in this house.
If we stopped to list them
and celebrate each one over again
the walls would once again ring and laugh
as they did each time before.
Most of the people I celebrate
still live here.
A list of them is unnecessary

Since you celebrate them daily even now.
Most of what I wish
is that the celebrations would continue.
And that I might have a hat always held for me
and a place set even if I'm late
and that my laughter might still
be held within these walls
on certain days.
Most of what I love is you
though not all
And I celebrate daily inside
other walls that surround me
That you taught me love and celebration
and helped me go forth to plan my own
festivals.

Maybe that is a little much because it was Christmas and I doubt we did as good as the credit he was giving. But even if we failed, Peggy and I wanted desperately to teach our children to laugh and celebrate and go forth to "plan their own festivals."

Recently the pastor and his family took a vacation during the break in school between Christmas and New Year's. He was gracious to ask me to speak on the Sunday he was absent. During the first service when the ushers came forward to bring the collection plates, one of them signaled me and I leaned forward. He handed me a note. It was from Peggy and it was written on one of her deposit slips. She always has plenty of those when the checks are gone. The note said:

Four years ago today you and I
didn't know if you would be here.
How's that for a Happy New Year?
I love you and believe in you.
                    Peg

I was in the hospital awaiting the results of surgery at the time to which she was referring. In the interval of waiting we had clung to each other as tight as we possibly could. But we had also let each other go. In these four years we have had one another like never before. Let go.

If this deep truth of God becomes meaningful in the deepest relationships of life, then how can we hold anything back from complete surrender to Him?

I was speaking at a retreat. Everybody was just spellbound, looking right at me. I was just kind of talking about this very thing—letting go—because it's been in my heart lately. I was thinking about it and talking about it a little, trying to explain it and not doing very well. All eyes were riveted on me. All of a sudden everybody's eyes went to the right and I was just standing there. So I looked over to see what was going on. And there were some walnut leaves that were blowing off the trees out there, floating down to the earth. I don't know how you say that. It wasn't a *herd* of leaves. I don't know what you call it. There were a bunch of them, enough to attract all those people's attention.

At that opportune time they came floating down by .

the window and I said, "Let's just be quiet for a minute. Everybody be quiet and don't say anything. Listen." They listened, wondering what I was up to. I said, "Did anybody hear the walnut tree complain?" Not a one of us did. The walnut tree just wasn't complaining at all.

Somewhere back down the line, God had said to the walnut tree, "If those leaves stay on all winter, then one night there will come a hard freeze and the temperature will drop. All that water will freeze on those leaves. It will snow and they will get so heavy it will break all of your limbs. It would be better if you would just let go of those leaves in the fall. I'll give you some more in the spring."

The walnut tree just said, "Okay." It just dropped those leaves. You ought to at least be as smart as a tree.

Do you have something you're just kind of hanging on to? Some little pet gripe? Maybe you're just hanging on to it because you like to hear people say, "Poor baby," once in a while. Just this moment could you say to the Lord, "Thank you for my job, my family and my possessions. They all belong to You."

In your mind turn the corner and ride down the street to your house. Look at your yard. The oak trees have grown, haven't they? Remember how small they were when you planted them? Go into the house and look at the things that make it your house. The way the rooms are decorated, the pictures. Remember when you bought the television? Isn't the carpet nice? Finally you bought new dining room furniture. The set you inherited when you got married has at last been moved to the playroom.

Go upstairs and look around. In the closets— the clothes, the ties, the shoes, the shirts and the skirts. Look out the window at your car and maybe your boat in the driveway. Go through your kids' rooms and see all the junk they've put on the walls - the pictures in the ball outfits and camp uniforms.

Go sit down in your favorite chair now and think of all the people and relationships that mean so much to you. Think about your office and all your hopes and fears and ambitions.

Now can you put it all into your open hands? Can you imagine all that is you and yours in your hands? Then the hard question for us all comes to mind. Can you hold it all with open hands, or must you grasp and hold? Is there something or someone that you feel you just have to at least keep a thumb on?

I wish for you the joy of holding life with an open hand. Just let go of all the stuff you've had to worry about and hang on to and protect, and drag, and fight everybody else away from. If you could just believe that you could hold them open. He'll help you with your marriage. He'll help you with your kids. He'll help you with your hopes and your dreams.

Chapter Eight

Chapter Eight

I Know *You*

Bill Gaither and I were sitting on the edge of the darkened stage as the second Praise Gathering for Believers was about to begin. Over six thousand people were in the audience. Even with the lights from the exit signs, the auditorium was almost totally black.

From the back of the auditorium Doug Oldham began to sing. The people quieted down to hear Doug's warm voice as he slowly sang his way toward the front. About halfway down the aisle the spotlights caught him. He stopped and, in the midst of that expectant throng, he continued to sing.

When Doug finished singing he was going to introduce Bill and me. We were to welcome everyone to Indianapolis for what we hoped and prayed would be

days of life-changing worship and praise. Neither of us
was too certain about what he was going to say and
each of us was graciously deferring to the other.

Doug finished and gave us the microphone and the
spotlights were on us. We began to try to welcome the
people. We were just having some fun with the
audience when I remembered something I had seen
Chico Holliday do at a great evening of music in
California a few months earlier.

I asked the people to identify themselves. "All the
Methodists, say 'Methodists' together." Then I called,
in turn, for Baptists, Presbyterians, Lutherans,
Nazarenes, Church of Goders, Pentecostals—down
through a list of all the groups I could call to mind.

Then I asked that everyone call out the name of his
group at the same time. On a signal everyone identified
his church. It came out something like

Baptodistyrianazalutheranevepenschurchofgod.

Some groups are a little more active in their worship
and they sounded out the strongest. But apparently
some people from the more reserved groups had
gotten some practice at basketball games or somewhere. They were not to be outdone. It was one more
confusing sound of Babel.

After the confusion died down I asked the audience
to say "Jesus." When we spoke His name together
there was such a unity that you could hardly believe
the beauty. Bill said, "Let's whisper it together." That
was the prettiest sound I think I've ever heard. "Jesus."

Jesus is the name which unites us and makes us one.
When we all speak at once the names of doctrines

which divide us, it comes out in a word that nobody understands. We create a sort of religious shouting and shoving match. Hardly anyone other than the shouters and shovers is interested in the contest.

When we say His name together we make a beautiful sound which becomes

Music in our ears—
the sweetest name on Earth.

We don't all say the name of Jesus alike. On almost back-to-back programs on the radio you hear various preachers say "Jesus." They each say His name in such a different way that you wonder if they are all saying the same word. Some have perfumed pronunciation that comes out smoothly like "Je-suzz." Isn't that lovely? Just hang on the "suzzz." "Je-suzzz." It makes Him sound so warm and sweet.

The next program is hosted by some good old-time preacher who is proclaiming the gospel as if he were fighting bees. He makes the name of Jesus a three-syllable word as he shouts out "Je-sus-aahh!" with great, moist emphasis on the "aahh!"

Regardless of how we speak the name of Jesus, it is the word which must be spoken. It is the one name which, when lifted up, draws all men in the same direction.

I have been writing to you about some of the great exciting things which are indelibly inscribed into the world about us and written in our hearts. We have been using terms like "secret" and "life" and "union." But we cannot relate ourselves to secrets or to unions or to life itself. The relationship is to a person—Jesus.

Jesus came to express God as a person because persons can love one another. Ideas and doctrines can prove. Climactic acts of nature can frighten. Events can become watersheds in history. Only persons can love.

We are instructed to "live our life in union with Him." The meaning does not come in understanding the great principles in life. It comes in our relationship to the personhood of God—Jesus.

I would like to borrow a phrase from John Powell: "Get to know Jesus." He alone is the source of life. In Him you will find your "portion of reality." It is in Him that you come to "a secure place in the human community." Henry David Thoreau wrote: "Dwell as near as possible to the channel in which your life flows."

On one of our end-of-the-summer short trips we went up into Virginia to the valley where the famous old Homestead Hotel is located. One afternoon Mike, Leigh, Tom, Patrick and I decided that we would climb the mountain and look out over the valley. We got a trail map of the area, drove to the foot of the trail and started up.

As we walked we began to hear the rushing of a mighty stream. We rounded a curve or two and came upon a huge tank. It was being filled by water which flowed from a pipe some two feet in diameter. The cold, clear mountain water gushed forth from that pipe. It flowed out of the bottom of that tank into another pipe which continued down into the valley.

We continued up the trail and switched back and forth across the face of the mountain. We saw several tanks like the first one, but each was smaller than the one below it. They were all alike in that each fed into a pipe which flowed to form the huge stream we had seen at the bottom of the mountain.

When we were nearly to the top of the mountain we saw a tank no larger than a wash pan. A one-inch pipe just trickled water into it. We followed that small pipe until it ended under some rocks. Hidden there was a tiny spring out of which flowed cool, clear, pure mountain water.

Whatever our capacity for greatness or service, far up in the headwaters of our hearts there must be the cool, clear stream of life.

A lot of what is done in the church is done by training, imagination, ideas, promotions, and various other gifts and gimmicks that are available to us. But one does not imitate life. It comes from one true source.

> *For some people, religion is like an artificial limb.*
> *It has neither warmth nor life.*
> *And although it helps them to stumble along,*
> *It never becomes a part of them.*
> *It must be strapped on each day.*

Again, let me remind you: Get to know Jesus. Until you do, all the rest is form and ceremony that will sometimes bless you and sometimes bore you half to death. He brings the Life. Get to know Jesus.

He is a person. The Christian religion is not a body of beliefs or creeds or ideals or truths. It is the person of

Christ. Our relationship to Christ is not a series of exams or tests or service categories such as Junior and Senior out of which we will finally be properly hooded and awarded doctoral degrees.

Nor is knowing Jesus like working some crossword puzzle. We do not eventually finish and cast it aside. He is a person and knowing Him is a growing, deepening, learning, loving, knowing journey on which we have embarked.

There will be beginning days when you think that perhaps it is just the gardener you hear. But the longer you walk together the more certain you are that the whisper you hear is His voice, that the touch on your shoulder is His touch, that the footsteps beside you are the coming of His feet.

> **One day He will come—**
> **once in the stillness**
> **you will know.**
> **Not from a book**
> **or the word of someone else**
> **but through Him.**

If you were with me in the upstairs sitting room and one of the family was coming up the steps, I would know who it was. You would say, "That must be an elephant." But I would know it was Patrick running with the dog.

Leigh was waiting at the beauty shop for the first haircut of her teens. It was not without some soul searching that she had decided to give up the long hair which reached down her back for a style which would be easier to keep up. Now she only needs two hours to get ready.

As she waited there she wrote me a letter. She told me that she was communicating with me "one more time" before she "changed." She quickly tired of writing so the letter was mostly a set of pictures drawn down the edge of the sheet. They were entitled:

"Things I Think About When I Think Of Dad"
(Not necessarily in that order)

First, she drew a racquet and ball and wrote "Tennis." "Mother" was second. I'm glad Leigh noted "not necessarily in that order." Peg's picture didn't come off quite as good as the tennis racquet. Next was the "New English Bible." You have probably observed by now that it is my favorite edition of the Bible. Tom calls it my NEB. Then there was "Laughter in the Walls" with walls which had "Ha, ha" written all over them. On down the page were "Lighthouses at Nantucket" and "The Rofero in Canada."

I'll have to tell you about the Rofero Hotel. We arrived in Quebec City in a rainstorm and everyone except the young boys and I wanted to go shopping. We wanted to ride the ferry and visit the fort. Before the shoppers left they instructed us to find a "far out" place to stay. None of the Holiday Inn stuff in this French speaking city.

Tom, Patrick and I went down a back street and found a three-story, walkup hotel. The Rofero had about four rooms and one bathroom on each floor. It was truly "far out." The hotel is a joke at our house now, but it wasn't too funny then. And I'll tell you something else. No one has ever asked me to find a "far out" place to stay again, either.

Leigh's other drawings included "clowns on the walls." I have a collection of clown pictures in my office. She also drew "hungry rabbits"—the ones the boys always forgot to feed—and "pineapple juice," for all vacations should have an ice chest full of canned juices. Just before she finished her artwork she drew "outstretched arms"—my gesture when I'm so happy I don't know what else to do—and "a stalled tractor." Machinery has always had it in for me.

Now I know that none of these things brings the picture to your mind that it does to us. It took years of living to put meaning into them for our family. That living involved work, play, traveling, fun and bad times. Out of our experiences together Leigh had a list of things she thought of when she thought of me.

What is it you think of when you think of Jesus? Certainly John 3:16. But do you think of times and places and moments and hours and words and touches and graces and sweetnesses? Is He mixed into the living of your life? Do you remember bedside vigils and Christmas dinners; vacations and rest; work and exhaustion? Is there a deepening bond between you and Him? Get to know Jesus.

Sometimes people know more about Jesus the day they meet Him than they ever will again. Occasionally I hear people testify, "I'm saved and I love Him. Pray for me." That's okay, except that is what they have been saying for thirty years.

What about you? Hasn't He done anything for you recently that is too good to keep to yourself? Isn't there some fresh word or some new insight that He has given? Hasn't a verse in the Bible leaped off the page and into your heart even though you had read it a thousand times before?

As you look back do you remember times when you were all alone and He was there? Did He ever laugh with you— maybe at something you did that was so crazy there was nothing else to do but laugh? Does He cry with you?

We should know Him so well from the past that we have the courage for today and optimism for tomorrow. Our relationship with Jesus is to be like that of most trusted friend. The longer that friendship exists, the richer its meaning and the more it becomes worth putting other things aside for.

"Get to know Jesus" is not a phrase which means to learn more facts or to devise a more intricate theological framework. It means getting to better know a friend.

My friend, Gary Paxton, is—as he will witness—a miracle of God's grace. He wrote a song entitled "Second-hand Faith." The refrain says:

Second-hand faith won't get you into heaven.
Some people never even get that close. All they know is that they heard someone else say that they heard another person mention something about what they remembered hearing from somebody a long time ago somewhere. By the time the news got to them so much

was "lost in the translation" that it hardly meant anything at all.

George Keith was probably a student of the Word of God. But somehow I feel that he is not reciting a collection of proof texts or repeating what he had heard someone else say when he wrote:

> *How firm a foundation, ye saints of the Lord,*
> > *is laid for your faith in His excellent Word,*
> *What more can he say than to you He hath said,*
> > *to you who for refuge to Jesus have fled?*
>
> *Fear not, I am with thee, oh, be not dismayed*
> > *for I am thy God I will still give thee aid.*
> *I'll strengthen thee, help thee, and cause thee to stand*
> > *upheld by my gracious, omnipotent hand.*
>
> *When through the deep waters I call thee to go*
> > *the rivers of sorrow shall not overflow,*
> *For I will be with thee, thy trials to bless*
> > *and sanctify to thee thy deepest distress.*
>
> *When thru fiery trials thy pathway shall lie*
> > *my grace all sufficient shall be thy supply*
> *The flames shall not hurt thee, I only design*
> > *thy dross to consume and thy gold to refine.*
>
> *E'en down to old age my people shall prove*
> > *my sovereign, eternal, unchangeable love.*
> *And when hoary hairs shall thy temples adorn*
> > *like lambs shall they still in my bosom be borne.*

The soul that on Jesus hath leaned for repose
I will not, I will not desert to his foes.
That soul, though all hell should endeavor to
*   shake*
I'll never, no never, no never forsake.

George Keith was writing out of a knowledge which only comes from friendship.

When I was of junior high school age there was a group of us at the church who had driven several men and women out of the Sunday School teaching profession. One by one, licking their wounds, they had gladly retreated to the peace and quiet of the couples' class.

We met in an old attic classroom that was furnished with seats taken from Nashville's newly defunct street car system. The backs of the seats still moved like they did when the car came to the end of the line. The motorman switched seats, attached the rear power pole and moved to the other end of the car to make it the front.

As soon as the teacher of that junior high class walked to the *front* of the room we promptly reversed the seats and left him at the rear of the coach. Finally, my Dad was appointed teacher of the class. That act in itself took care of the behavior of one class member. He promptly went to work on the others.

He suggested that one weekend we go to Ruskin Cave in West Tennessee to camp out. There were some old buildings there which were left over from the days when a college was located there. Dad had attended the school for a year or so and he was anxious to get close to us by taking us through the cave and swimming in Yellow Creek.

The closer the time for us to take the trip came, the less Dad relished going off by himself with that crowd of boys. He invited some of the couples in the church and prevailed on Mom to go along to cook. He persuaded the pastor to come and speak. Ruskin Cave Camp Meeting was born. That camp meeting was only held for a few years but there are some great memories from those days in a lot of people's hearts.

We held the services in the cave. It was "air conditioned" before anyone knew what air conditioning was. Over thirty years ago a close friend of mine, Don Irwin, was speaking in the afternoon service. I went forward and knelt in the straw at an old rough bench and dedicated my life to the Lord and to whatever He wanted me to do.

Just outside the cave there was a fountain that just bubbled up all the time with cold, clear water coming out from under that Tennessee limestone hillside. I'm certain that on that hot, dusty August afternoon I got a drink as I went into service and another when I came out.

Over the span of those years some wonderful things have happened to me. I have also had some moments of abject discouragement. But the vow I made that afternoon has been lifelong.

Tom asked us one night if it is true that God always wants you to do "what you don't want to do the most." I suppose everyone wonders at times if His ways are good ways. Is He really like a shepherd who "leads beside the still waters" or is He some arbitrary crank who had this uncanny way of making pianists play left guard and fullbacks cut paperdolls?

A couple of months ago I was speaking at a retreat in West Tennessee. Tom, Patrick and I took the pickup truck and our Hondas. The retreat site was only about twenty miles from Ruskin, so after the Saturday morning service we drove over to see the old camp meeting site. We walked over the grounds and got a drink from the fountain which was still bubbling forth—as crystal clear as ever.

We went into the cave and I showed them how we had set up the chairs and benches to make a place for the services. I pointed to the spot where the choir had stood as Dad led the singing. I showed them the place where I knelt when I made that vow. I told them, as best I could, that just as surely as that fountain still gave forth clear, pure water, His grace and goodness flooded and filled my being that morning just as it had so many years before.

We put on our helmets and rode away. As we did, I was praying that I had answered a little bit of Tom's question. Thirty years—and if it had changed at all it only tasted better. Get to know Jesus.

I was preaching down in Florida recently. I really thought that I was laying the truth out so precisely and powerfully that when I finished, there would be no need for additions, deletions, or corrections. When the service was over a most distinguished black lady came to me and told me that her name was Olive and that she was seventy-four years old. With great kindness she let me know that what one can learn about Jesus in thirty years couldn't begin to compare with all He had come to mean in "three score and ten." "You're just beginning to get to know Jesus, son."

I'm certain there will always be mystery and awe about Him. But we must begin our journey with Him— the journey which will someday lead us to the Father's house. Remember, He is the very Life of life.

Edna St. Vincent Millay reminds us that, when we finally meet Him face to face, the thing which will surprise us the most is how often we have seen Him before. We will not be saying, "Oh, I thought your hair would be longer." We won't be thinking that we had imagined that He talked with a deeper voice.

Instead, we will be saying, "I know *you*. I remember *you*. I've seen you a thousand times. I know *you*." And He will say, "Yes, I know you, too. I know you, too."

There is a musical based on the novel, "The Yearling," by Marjorie Rawlings. In that musical there is a song—"My Pa"— which tells in lovely verse some of

the richness of knowing an earthly father. It also
captures some of what it can mean to get to know
Jesus:

> *My Pa can light my room at night*
>> *with just his being here*
> *And make a fearful dream alright*
>> *by grinning ear to ear.*
> *My Pa can do most anything*
>> *he sets his mind to do.*
> *He'd even move a mountain*
>> *if he really wanted to.*
> *My Pa can sweeten up a day*
>> *that clouds and rain make gray*
> *And tell me funny stories*
>> *that will chase the clouds away.*
> *My Pa's the only one on earth*
>> *I can tell my troubles to*
> *His arms are house and home to me*
>> *his face a pretty poem to me.*
> *My Pa's the finest friend I ever knew*
>> *I only wish that you could know him, too.*

Chapter Nine

Creation is Complete—The Godhead is Complete—
The Church is Complete—Two Something's Deeper—
Too Much Dive—Please Forgive Me—I'll Take Number Six—
Being Pure, Seeing God—Seeing God, Being Pure

Chapter Nine

But I'm Not Pure

If those who knew me were to try to describe me with one word which would portray me to those who didn't know me, I wonder what word they would use. I'm not really certain I would like to hear the list, but at least I know some of the words they wouldn't use. "Complete" is not one of the words they might choose. "Inadequate," "late," "noncommunicative," "in-the-process," "struggling," and perhaps even "earnest or "sincere"they might choose, but not "complete."

The ideas of being brought to fulfillment and being thoroughly finished and the words "complete" and "completeness" are strong in Paul's thinking as he writes to his brothers in the church at Colossae. In fact, the ideas are so rich and deep that you can almost see

Paul's hand racing to keep up with his mind as he writes. The Colossians were people who had heard of Christ through Epaphras, a fellow servant of Paul's. Paul describes him as "dear."

In this letter Paul begins to remind them of all that is brought to completion in Christ Jesus. He is grateful that **". . . the message . . . is coming to men the whole world over . . . and everywhere it is growing and bearing fruit as it is doing among them."**

These great verses in the first and second chapters of Colossians indicate that it is in Christ that creation finds its completion. **"In Him everything in heaven and on earth was created. . . He exists before everything. . . all things are held together in Him."**

Every step He ever took was upon ground that He Himself had made. Every cup of water that He ever put to His lips was formed of droplets of water that He had brought into being. Every heart to which He gently spoke was alive with the breath of His life. The great cycles of creation find their wholeness in Him.

Paul also writes, **"In Him, the complete being of God came to dwell . . . in Him the complete being of the Godhead dwells embodied. . ."**

Great is the God who creates a world of dust and dirt. Greater still is He who comes to dwell within it. So that we may know that He is God, He became man. The one who made us now comes to walk among us.

To look us in the face
to take us by the hand

To wipe our weeping eyes
to tell us of our Father
and His love for us.

Jesus, our Creator, the "primacy over all things," becomes Jesus, our Brother, "the embodiment of the Godhead . . ." Man can begin to understand God in His completeness.

Paul is also saying that Christ is the completeness of the church. **"He is, moreover, the head of the body, the church. He is its origin, the first to return from the dead, to be in all things alone supreme."**

I was riding up through Idaho recently for a weekend retreat. After we had turned off the interstate, we began to go through little towns with populations like 782. I saw little churches like the ones I had pastored a long time ago. I was reminded of many of the frustrations and struggles of those days. I wondered if my dedication is deep enough to take me back to one of those little places again. I wondered what it would be like to be without Peg. Oh, I'm sure she would go, but God gets to tell her. I also secretly hoped that God realized that I am far too important for something like that now.

As we were returning, after an early Sunday morning retreat service, we went back by those tiny churches. Parked along side of each of those little concrete block or frame buildings there were about six pickup trucks, a couple of old cars and sometimes one Lincoln for the guy who owns the funeral home.

In my mind I could see squirming little boys in Sunday School classes who were now grown men and had moved away to Seattle or Portland. They were working now to raise their own families. Most of the values and principles that give their lives any permanence at all were imparted in those little churches. I could see Moms and Dads, older now and alone since the family had gone, climb out of those trucks. They went to services to pray earnestly for their sons and daughters and grandkids who were hundreds of miles away in busy, complex societies.

I thought of Paul's words about the church being complete in Christ. The church has often had its problems. At times it even seems to have lost its way. Sometimes its voice is muted and only adds questions to questions. But He is the head of the church and in Him it finds its completion.

All of these good things are not hard for me to believe and accept. To believe that **"all that came to be was alive with His life"** will compute for me. To read the gospels and hear His words and see His deeds makes me to know that He who sees Jesus has indeed seen the Father and that They are One. The sturdy fabric of the church stretches and holds widely diverse opinions and interpretations. It continues to function as the great vehicle of truth in spite of the weaknesses and foibles of those who lead it.

I must confess to you that the next step in Paul's progression of thought is one which makes me pause. For now he writes ". . . and in Him you have been brought to completion." Whatever else we are "Completion ain't one of our weaknesses." Between knowing me and watching you, it is hard for me to decide who is farther from completeness.

Do you feel complete today? Do you feel adequate? Do you pray enough? Are you kind enough? Do you forgive grudges quickly enough? Does your life have power? Does it have meaning? Do you live up to your own dreams and hopes and expectations? Or do you approach Paul's affirmation that "you have been brought to completion" hoping with me that in a rich, deep beauty it applies to us in some way that we have not yet discovered or fathomed?

We believe that He is the fulfillment of these other great, wonderful processes and purposes of God. Now we must come in trust and confidence to know that our wholeness is also "in Him."

I am realizing more and more that, if I am ever to get to a place where I am whole, or real, or complete, I will first have to be lifted and forgiven from all the partial, stumbling, half-hearted, half-accomplished deeds, misdeeds and "undones" of the past. I am an accumulation of guilts, pains, memories, scars, failures and sins of the past.

I suppose incompleteness is the only area in which I am really full-orbed. I was thinking of this when I wrote some lines which I called "Multiple Me's":

Most of the time it seems there
is just not enough of me
to go around.

At the office it is almost as
    if I leave more to do than
    I am ever able to get done.
And when I'm home—the yard,
    the family, the woodpile,
    the garage all seem to have a
    rightful claim on my time.
All of the projects that I would
    like to be able to begin—
    the books I would like to read—
    could all be done if there
    were only more of me to do them.

But then there are times when
    there are just
        too many of me.
One of those times is when I pray.
If only Bob, the sincere, the
    quiet, the desirer of holy
        things, could make his way
        alone to the place of prayer
    and make his petitions known,
    and there find the
        power and poise
    his heart must have.
But every time he goes to pray
    a whole multitude of me's comes
    trooping right along—
        Bob the impatient,
    Bob the referee heckler,

Bob the unconcerned,
and the ambitious Bob
and the unkind Bob.

And by the time they all crowd
into the closet,
there is such a din
and clamor that
I can hardly hear
the voice of God.
And then I am made to see
that what I am —
in my thoughts
at work, at play,
in traffic —
all these people
make up the person I am
when I kneel down to pray.
Oh, that I would love Him so
dearly that every moment
of my life —
ease, thought, pain,
pleasure, toil, dreams —
would be but a preparation
for those times when
I shall be alone
with Him.

Before I can ever hope or dream to be something
else, I must be redeemed, forgiven, released from what
I was. Before I can think of genuineness for my todays
and greatness for my tomorrows, the ceilings from my

yesterdays will have to be lifted.

There are a couple of lovely pictures here that Paul paints for us. Before he steps to the canvas though, he boldly states ". . . he has forgiven us all our own sins; he has cancelled the bond which . . . stood against us."

Our failures and our sins **". . . He discarded like a garment . . . and . . . nailed it to the cross."** It is as if He took all of the bad of all of your yesterdays and stuck them into his coat pocket and hung it on the crossarm of the cross. They thought they were nailing Him to a tree. Paul says He was nailing all the decrees and authorities and cosmic powers **". . . to rescue us from the domain of darkness and bring us into the kingdom."**

The other picture is even more vivid to me. It is easy to see yourself surrounded by the habits and failures that dog your footsteps. In spite of all your resolutions, new starts, and fresh beginnings, you seem powerless to shake them. Your temper, your spirit, your bitterness, your sarcasm, your pettiness seem to come and go as they will.

Paul says that **"he made a public spectacle of them and led them as captives in His triumphant procession."** In His forgiveness all the things that seemed like your captors, are led along as prisoners themselves. You are on the sidewalk, cheering the One who set you free.

In our Sunday School class one morning we were talking about the depth of the love of God. How deep is His love? How deep will it really go?

Someone said, "It goes as deep as you go." I said,

"Well, that's okay, except I want to add another phrase if you don't mind." Since I had the microphone and I was the teacher they said, "Okay, you can add another phrase." "I want to say it goes as deep as you go and two somethings deeper." I don't care what. Two inches, two feet, two miles, just two somethings. It is just always down there below you.

I have a friend whom I know casually. I had met him a time or two before. I saw him again toward the end of one summer. He was wearing a neck brace and was kind of hunched up. He didn't look like he was having much fun that day.

I took counseling in seminary so I know how to get stuff out of people. Using my professional counseling techniques I said, "Did your wife hit you?" No response. So I went into a deeper, more probing statement: "You thought they said 'Stand up' when they said 'Shut up'." That didn't elicit any response either so finally I said, "Aw, come on. Tell me what happened."

"Well, I'm kind of embarrassed to, but I will. My son and I were up the street at the neighbors who have a new swimming pool. They had invited us to swim and we were diving off the board. I really hate to tell you this, but I hit my head on the bottom. Really, it knocked me out. If my son hadn't been there to bring me to the surface and drag me up on the wall, I probably would have drowned."

I have a quick mind—like a steel trap. You've noticed that, I know. Right away, I knew what had happened to him. I didn't share this precious truth with him, although I knew the scientific principle involved. He had run out of water before he ran out of dive. He looked like he knew it.

For whatever it is that plagues you—maybe some deep, dark deed that would startle and shock us all, maybe a steady accumulation of the same thing—I want to write this very plainly. There are always two somethings deeper still. Forgiveness is not forgiveness unless it is unconditional. *He forgives.*

One night I came in very late. The family was all in bed. On the table in the playroom by the door in a puddle of light from an overhead lamp was a note. It was a little like a poster because there was some artwork on it. It said:

> **Dear Dad,**
> **I did something bad today.**
> **I am sorry. Please forgive**
> **me.**
>
> > **Tom**

Tom has a little of the con man in him, too, because it also said:

> **P.S.—I love you.**

It doesn't matter what time I get home. I always make the rounds to kiss my family and whisper to their sleeping forms that I love them. This night I stopped by Patrick first. He is always as warm as toast. He usually says groggily, "Goodnight," in a kind of a "keep moving" tone. Then into Leigh's room. She is a responder. Whatever you say to her she will say back. "I love you, Leigh." "I love you, too, Dad," "You sure

are a fine daughter." "You are a fine dad, too." It's hard
to leave such lovely conversations as this.

Next I went into Tom's room. Tom doesn't ever
wake up or even answer. He sits up in the bed so
quickly after you kiss him that you have to duck to
keep from getting hit. It took a moment to get him back
on his pillow and to put the covers up under his chin.
He still didn't even know I was there. Kneeling by his
bed, I said softly into his unhearing ear, "Tom, you are
forgiven."

Someone asked how I could forgive when I didn't
even know what he had done yet. It is really simple. He
can't do anything for which I won't forgive him. He has
"blanket" coverage. You do not have to carry the
weight of your past into your tomorrows. You can step
through the door of forgiveness. But completeness
seems to me to be more than just getting over what I
was. It has something to do with what I am becoming.

In the Sunday School class we've been studying the
Beatitudes. I don't know why, but it makes me feel
better educated or smart or something not to use the
quarterly lessons. I just always feel smug or something
just winging away on my own. I'm not sure this is any
great blessing to the Director of Christian Ed or to the
Sunday School Superintendent. This may be part of
the joy. So we've been studying the Beatitudes.

The sixth Beatitude seems to stand out to me above
all the rest. First of all, it stands out in terms of its great
promise. Now, there are other promises in the

Beatitudes. The Beatitudes themselves are a series of statements or conditions and corresponding rewards and promises. When you put all the promises together "the kingdom of heaven is theirs;" "consolation;" "they shall have the earth for their possession;" "they shall be satisfied;" "mercy shall be shown to them;" "God shall call them His sons;" or again, "the kingdom of heaven is theirs," it just seems to me that the richest promise of them all is contained in the words, "They shall see God." I'd rather see God than possess the earth. I'd just take a chance on finding enough satisfaction and enough mercy and enough consolation if I could just see Him.

On Christmas night a group of us have a custom of getting together. One of the good things about our gathering has been that we get rid of the leftover turkey. But the fellowship is always good, too. This year it was at someone else's house and her mother was there.

We had known the mother for a long time. She was unusually quiet that evening. We thought it was because she had always been a very busy, active person and always had schedules to meet. There were people depending on her. Now she was retired after some 30 years of having to be at school, to teach and to grade papers. She just didn't seem to feel like a whole lot depended on her anymore. We thought that maybe that was the reason she was sad.

I talked to her a lot that evening. It just happened that as I moved around I kept coming back to sit beside her. She was talking about being homesick for heaven, about seeing God. I guess if I were to ask how many of you were homesick for heaven you would all say, "Yes, I'm homesick for heaven." I also know that if I said, "We're taking the church bus and we're going right away," there would be room for everyone who wanted to go.

A few days after Christmas our retired friend learned that she had an inoperable cancer. Her days probably could now be numbered. It is sad and rather strangely tragic that when she had finally finished her life work there was not going to be much time left for rest and visiting her children and grandchildren. But it is also somehow deeply reinforcing to me to know that the longer the trip the deeper the desire to make it home. This promise becomes more precious: "They shall see God."

If the sixth Beatitude holds forth the greatest promise, it also seems to have the greatest obstacle. "How blessed are those whose hearts are pure." Now we may be poor or poor in spirit. Most of the time life takes care of that. Heaven knows we will be sorrowful. Maybe from time to time we may even develop within ourselves a gentle spirit. In quiet, pensive moments I think we all hunger and thirst for righteousness. Now and then we can even find mercy in our hearts, especially when we remember in the Lord's Prayer that we will find mercy in the same measure that we bestow it. I think we are even peacemakers if the cause doesn't matter much to us either way. Most of us suffer some persecution, and even though not much is for the cause of right, we tell everybody it is and feel better about it. All of these things we are into in some measure. We might have some chance of attaining enough merit in these areas to qualify for the reward.

But here is this monstrous door which seems to have a lock to which we have no key. Standing between us and seeing God is the qualification "Blest are those whose hearts are pure." Which of us is pure? I wouldn't stand before you and say I was pure because you wouldn't believe me. It wouldn't be true. I don't meet many people who are pure, either.

It's always a little easier to speak away from home. You can get a couple of hundred miles away from home and you can look more pure than you do at home. You just meet with the people for such a short time. In three days they can't find out much about you. I just happen to be one who cries a lot when I talk, and when you cry people think you are pure. People say, "My , my, isn't he fine!", as long as you don't get mixed up in all the retreats and get in the volleyball games and stuff like that where you might cheat or lose your temper. Go to your room and they'll think you're studying and praying and that you're saintly when you are really just taking a nap. It's easy to look pure.

I would like to get to the place where I could go somewhere and talk to people and say to them: "Hey, come on, way up here where I am. The view is great. The air is clean and pure. If you could just be up here where I am." But I always seem to be puffing and sweating and blowing and walking along the trail with everyone else and saying: "Hey, there it is, way up there. Way up there is where we ought to be."

I really think I'm getting old enough to be pure. I've been at this for thirty years. You would think that sooner or later I might turn up pure. It really doesn't matter if I'm two hundred miles from home or two thousand miles from home or at home. I'm still me. I'm still what I am. I know the gap between what I am and what I ought to be. I'm not pure. I'm always plagued by what I am.

So I come back to the phrase, **"In Him you have been brought to completion."** How blessed are those whose hearts are pure, for they shall see God. But I'm a tenacious fellow. I don't give up too easily. Lately, I have a feeling about the Word. There's a lot of stuff there. If you keep looking into the Word there must be something there that will help you.

I had always taken the phrase "How blessed are those who are pure in heart, for they shall see God" to mean that at some time in judgment some minor official will open my heart, look in and say, "You're not pure so you can't see God."

Here I am wanting to see God. Here I am without a pure heart. Here is the verse which says, "In Him I have been brought to completion." I'm looking for a way to put these three things together.

"I want to see God."

"But you're not pure."

"I have to see God."

"But you have to be pure."

"I need to see God."

"But you need to be pure."

I wasn't getting anywhere starting at the front, so I went around to the back door. One day a voice within me said:

"I have seen God."

"Then you must be pure."

"I have heard His voice. I have seen His ways."

"Then you must be pure."

"In Him you have been brought to completion."

Every time you say to me that I am not complete I'm going to say, "I agree, but . . . He said I was."

There is a lady in our church and I am ashamed to confess that I only know three things about her. First, her name is Rose. Second, she always sits on the right side of the middle section on the first or second pew. Third, every time there is a call for prayer, an invitation song or a concluding song, Rose goes to the altar to pray. This is all that I know about her.

Peg and I were wondering one day about how the Lamb's Book of Life would look if it depended on Rose's faith and trust. Her name would be on every page an average of three times. It would look like this:

> Sam
> Richard
> Wilhemina
> *Rose*
> Charles
> Alice

John
Mary
Rose
Pauline
Tracey
Keith
Lucas
Rose

I can hear someone now saying, "Who is this *Rose?*"

I'll tell you one thing I would like to see. There is a place I would like to be standing. It may be some Sunday morning at the church. I surely hope I haven't retreated somewhere. It may be when Rose gets to the Gate. Her face always seems tinged with just a little sadness and struggle. I would like to be there to see her face break into a smile that would eclipse a sunrise on a summer morning when she finally hears for the first time —

"*Rose* —
   You are all right,
   You are just O. K.,
   Everything is fine.
You are complete."

I know three things about Rose and I know three things about you. First, well, I have forgotten your name but, *ooh,* that face. Second, I know that you have probably found your seat in life — over to the left side and four rows back. Third, I am almost certain that in your own strength you make as pathetic a figure as Rose, standing there in her frayed, grey, winter coat which is too heavy in spring and too light in winter.

No. Come to think of it I know four things about me, about Rose, about you—

"In Him we are brought to completion."